NEW ORLEANS
Classic
GUMBOS & SOUPS

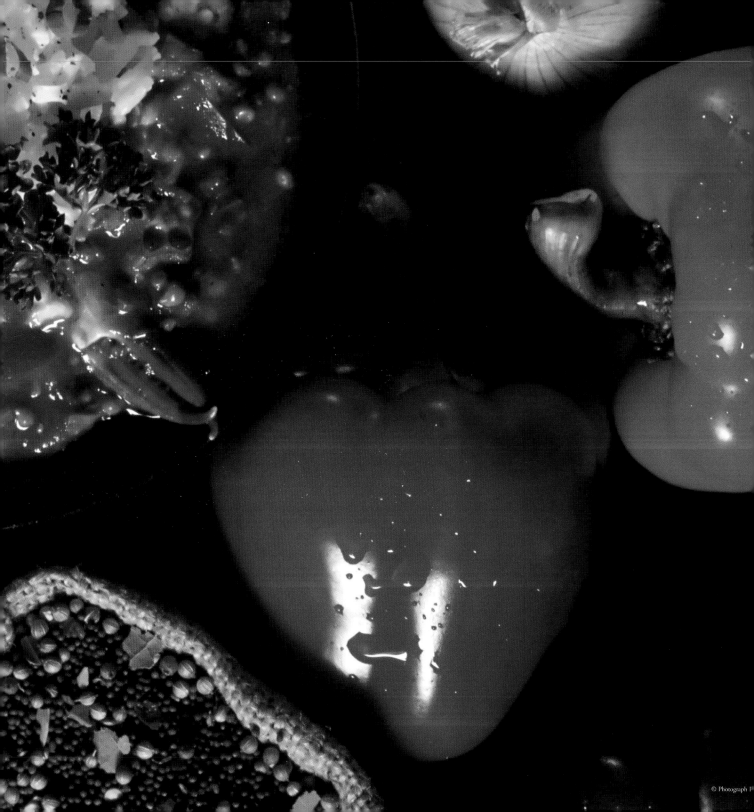

NEW ORLEANS

Classic

GUMBOS & SOUPS

Recipes from Favorite Restaurants

KIT WOHL

PELICAN PUBLISHING COMPANY

GRETNA 2009

"Creole Seafood Gumbo" recipe from *Galatoire's Cookbook (pages 14-15)* by Melvin Rodrigue and with Jyl Benson, copyright ©2005 by Galatoire's Restaurant. Used by permission of Clarkson Potter/Publishers, a division of Random House, Inc.

"Gumbo z'Herbes" recipt from *The Dooky Chase Cookbook (pages 52-53)* by Leah Chase, copyright ©1990 used by permission of the publisher, Pelican Publishing Company, Inc.

"Louisiana Seafood Okra Gumbo Classique" recipe from *The Frank Davis Seafood Notebook* (pages 258-259) by Frank Davis ©1983 used by permission of the publisher, Pelican Publishing Company, Inc.

Image of Frank Davis from cover of *Frank Davis Makes Good Groceries!* written by Frank Davis, photography by Mike Sanders, Visions Photography ©2008 used by permission of the publisher, Pelican Publishing Company, Inc.

For Linda Jane Ellerbee, who leads the parade.

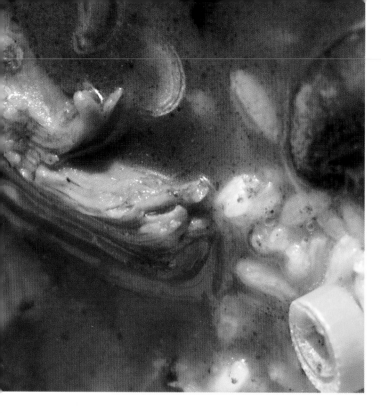

CONTENTS

Gumbo

Bisque

NEW ORLEANS
Words an
ANTOINE DOMINO
and RO

"You go messin' with my mama's gumbo, you gonna get hurt."

There are a lot of do's and don'ts in New Orleans. The first "do" is to learn how to make a roux. The second is not to mess with anybody's mama's gumbo recipe. Or if you do, lie about it because the process of preparing a gumbo can lead to arguments, duels and fanciful thinking. But that's okay. Fanciful thinking is no mystery in New Orleans. It's the way we do things.

Think streetcars swaying on tracks, grand oak trees, misty, murky bayous, joyous music, and flavor. Flavors to conjure with.

Take gumbo. Variations on the theme are endless, much as every piece of improvisational jazz is a musical celebration all its own.

The basic formula for making gumbo is simple. What's on hand? What's in season? Then make a stock, and cook flour in oil to make a roux. Celery, bell pepper and onion (aka the Louisiana cook's "holy trinity") are wilted in the roux, and the stock is seasoned. The meat, poultry or seafood is added, creating the flavor profile.

Making do was the foundation of both the Creole and the Acadian (or "Cajun," if you will) culinary cultures. It was make do then and it still is.

For citified Creoles, "making groceries" meant buying from street peddlers for some provisions, and visiting the French Market's stalls along the riverfront to purchase others. The country Cajuns lived in the bayous, rich with game and seafood, and went hunting and fishing as shopping expeditions.

The first Creole cooks, primarily from France, Africa, Spain or the Caribbean, often had no access to the kinds of fresh ingredients they were accustomed to using. So they improvised with different ingredients, using cooking techniques that may have been acquired thousands of miles from New Orleans.

Louisiana's multitude of traditional gumbos and soups are savory reflections of our cultural diversity and creativity.

A good gumbo is held in the highest regard. A courtbouillon may be the soup of kings, and here the monarchs are Mardi Gras kings.

Bisque is sheer elegance. Debutantes gracefully dip spoons into bowls of it, wearing long gowns, and elbow-length gloves, at the queen's Carnival breakfast following the ball.

For meals, everyone is royalty. We gather anywhere and everywhere for lunch or dinnertime gumbo or soup from either fine china or a plastic bowl. It is a most democratic dish, simmering through all strata of society.

Remember, most gumbos and soups weren't created by chefs in the first place. We want you to be happy, look good, create a wonderful recipe, and add your own magical good taste.

Preconceived notions can create surprises. Who knew that some gumbos do not use roux? Is it heresy or inspiration to serve sweet potatoes or potato salad instead of rice with gumbo? Or even a sweet potato salad?

No matter. Each dish has been home-kitchen tested by real people who are not chefs and are free with their opinions.

At bottom, the cuisines of the Creoles and the Cajuns are two aspects of a single, broad-ranging cooking style. At its best, it is not mere nourishment.

It's food that stirs you to dream of the next meal. And it's probably the greatest legacy of our Louisiana ancestors. Cooks borrowed from everywhere; they used what they had; they made everything work together.

Out of sheer appreciation—and appetite—we continue to follow their lead.

Because fanciful thinkin' still leads to mighty good eatin'.

–Kit Wohl

Gerard Maras's distinguished cooking career has taken him from his native upstate New York to the kitchens of such stellar New Orleans establishments as Commander's Palace, Mr. B's Bistro, Bacco and his own Gerard's Downtown. In the 1980s he led the movement among the city's restaurant chefs toward the use of super-fresh products grown on farms in the surrounding region.

These days, Gerard divides his time among several pursuits—making practical use of his culinary experience by working as a consultant, teaching classes in the mysteries of Creole cooking techniques, and harvesting and canning dew-fresh fruits and vegetables from a large rural garden of his own, which he tends alongside his wife, Tommy.

GERARD MARAS

CHICKEN AND OYSTER FILÉ GUMBO WITH BACON

In Creole cookery, as in almost every other cuisine, breaking a rule is not always a sin. Take, for example, this gumbo recipe's combination of meat and seafood. At first blush, it's a match-up of contradictory flavors. But one taste of the dish itself should convince many an open-minded eater that the resulting flavor is heavenly. Likewise, the absence of a roux does not diminish the down-home-Louisiana quality of chef Gerard Maras' delicious blend of chicken, oysters and bacon.

SERVES: 8

3 tablespoons	unsalted butter	2	garlic cloves, chopped
6 ounces	sliced bacon	2	whole bay leaves
1	fresh raw chicken, with bones removed, cut into 1- or 2-inch pieces	1 pint	raw oysters, with juices
		2 quarts	chicken stock*
		1 quart	water
2	large yellow onions, 1/4-inch dice	1/2 cup	flat-leaf (Italian) parsley, chopped
1	jalapeño pepper	1/2 cup	filé powder
1 tablespoon	dried thyme		kosher or sea salt, to taste
			freshly ground black pepper, to taste

*See page 85 for a chicken stock recipe.

DIRECTIONS

In a large soup pot, melt the butter. Cut the bacon slices in half and cook the pieces in the butter to render their fat and lightly brown them.

Add the chicken pieces a few at a time, turning to cook them evenly. Add the onions, jalapeño pepper, thyme, garlic and bay leaves. Sauté the mixture until the onions become transparent.

Strain the oysters over a mixing bowl, then pour the bowl of oyster juices into the pot with the sautéed chicken and seasonings. Stir everything well, scraping the bottom of the pot to be sure all ingredients are blended in.

Add the chicken stock and water and bring the liquid to a boil. Reduce heat to a moderate simmer.

Cook the gumbo for 1 hour. Then add the whole oysters and parsley and simmer for an additional 5 minutes. Season with salt and pepper to taste.

Just before serving time, bring the gumbo to a simmer and stir the filé into it. Remove from heat and serve in bowls with cooked rice and about a tablespoon or so of extra filé powder on the side, for those who'd like to add a pinch or two of it to the gumbo.

LENA RICHARD

Creole Gumbo Filé

Gumbo is usually served over rice. With a salad and hot French bread, there' is a no more satisfying meal.

SERVES: 4 to 6

4 tablespoons	vegetable oil	1 cup	raw chicken meat, medium-diced or cut into small pieces
1/2 pound	raw ham, medium diced	1	whole bay leaf
1 pound	raw shrimp shrimp small to medium, shelled	3 teaspoons	filé powder
3 tablespoons	all-purpose flour	1	garlic clove, chopped
1	medium-size onion, chopped		kosher or sea salt, to taste
1 1/2 quarts	chicken stock*		black pepper, freshly ground to taste
1 dozen	gumbo crabs**		

*See page 85 for a chicken stock recipe.
**Hard-shell crabs that are too small or scrawny to be picked for meat lumps.

DIRECTIONS

Before preparing this recipe, read the instructions for making roux on pages 86-87.

In a 5- or 6-quart Dutch oven (preferably made of cast iron) fry the ham and shrimp in the vegetable oil until the ham is a golden brown. Remove the ham and shrimp from the pot and set aside.

Add the flour to the remaining vegetable oil to begin making a roux, constantly stirring and blending the flour and oil until the flour reaches a medium to dark brown color. Just before the roux's color reaches that point, stir the chopped onion into the roux and cook them until the onion pieces become soft and semi-transparent, 5 to 10 minutes.

Add the chicken stock, crabs, shrimp, ham and diced chicken to the pot, as well as the bay leaf and chopped garlic. Cook on low-to-medium heat until the liquid is reduced to about 1 1/2 quarts.

Season to taste with salt and pepper. Just before serving, stir in the filé powder. Serve over cooked rice.

This recipe is based on one created by Lena Richard, one of New Orleans's best known caterers during the 1930s and '40s. It appears in her "New Orleans Cook Book," first published in 1940.

Richard's repertory encompassed virtually every classic dish in the Creole style. This gumbo, also known as "Creole filé gumbo," contains ham, shrimp, chicken and crabs. Others might contain oysters or bits of pork sausage in addition to, or instead of, the main ingredients used in this recipe.

In one version or another, this gumbo remains to this day one of the oldest and most authentic traditional dishes created by New Orleans' African-American cooks.

Galatoire's executive chef Brian Landry was crowned king of seafood by the Louisiana Seafood Promotion Board, a high honor that could be, in the restaurant world, almost as significant as being named king of Carnival.

Galatoire's is another of the famous grand Creole restaurants, now more than 100 years old. A vintage establishment often has traditions and secrets. Certainly no one gossips about it. They chat.

Waiters know regular guests' quirks, preferences, and who to seat, or not, next to whom. These services are almost as important as the secrets.

Following a martini or two, either yours or of those nearby, one can overhear which debutante is likely to be queen of carnival, what civic leader has been named Rex or king and queen of Comus. Either throne is the pinnacle of a coming out season or career.

Those are the nicer things waiting to be overheard. All of the rest are usually as delicious as the menu items.

CREOLE SEAFOOD GUMBO

Ask any dyed-in-the-wool New Orleanian to name a single dish that epitomizes the classic Creole style and odds are the answer will be a seafood gumbo with okra. In fact, the word "gumbo" itself is a variation of "quingombo," an old West African term for okra.

Slender, pale-green okra pods, sliced for cooking, are one of the two most essential thickening agents for a traditional gumbo. The other is filé, which is made by pounding sassafras leaves to a powdery consistency. Cooked okra imparts a subtle, unique flavor that somehow flatters the shrimp, crab and oyster flavors of this gumbo, which is regularly sent forth from the kitchen at Galatoire's Restaurant, which for more than a century has many of the oldest—and best—classics of the French-Creole style. A rich, dark roux provides structure for the dish.

SERVES: 10 to 12 (about 2 gallons)

2 cups plus 3 tablespoons	vegetable oil	3 dozen	raw oysters, shelled
3	whole bay leaves	2 pounds	okra, stems removed
1	large onion, diced (about 2 cups)	1 pound	jumbo lump crab meat, picked over
1 1/2 gallons	crab stock*	1 tablespoon	kosher sea salt
2	celery stalks, sliced (about 1 cup)	4 cups	all-purpose flour
		1 tablespoon	cayenne pepper
2 pounds	medium shrimp (45 to 50 per pound), shelled	2 cups	cooked white rice
		1 tablespoon	white pepper freshly ground
2 8-ounce cans	crushed tomatoes		

See page 85 for a crab stock recipe.

DIRECTIONS

Heat 3 tablespoons of the oil in a stockpot, then add the onion and celery. Sauté the vegetables over medium to high heat for 5 minutes, or until they are tender and the onions begin to brown.

Add the tomatoes and okra and simmer until the moisture has cooked out. Season with the salt, pepper and bay leaves and add the stock. Bring to a boil over high heat. Lower the heat to a simmer and add the shrimp, oysters and crab meat to the stock. Continue simmering for 10 minutes.

While the gumbo is simmering, make a roux in a cast-iron or other heavy frying pan. Place the pan over medium heat and then add the remaining two cups of oil and the flour to the pan, whisking until smooth. Continue to cook, whisking constantly, until the roux becomes a walnut color. If the pan starts to get too hot during the cooking process, remove it from the heat, still whisking, and allow to cool briefly. Be extremely careful not to burn the roux. Constant whisking will keep the roux from sticking.

Stir the brown roux into the soup a little at a time. When all of the roux has been incorporated, simmer the soup for about 10 minutes, until thickened. Remove the bay leaves. Ladle the gumbo into the soup plates or gumbo bowls and garnish with a large spoonful of rice.

© Photograph Cheryl Gerber

MATTHEW MURPHY, MÉLANGE
THE RITZ-CARLTON HOTEL, NEW ORLEANS

Duck Gumbo

SERVES: 6 to 8

1	Muscovy duck, about 2 1/2 pounds	1	large carrot, roughly chopped
	dark roux*	1/2 gallon	duck stock, made with duck bones
1 cup	duck fat from baking	1 tablespoon	vegetable oil
1 cup	all-purpose flour	2	garlic cloves, chopped
2 gallons	water	1 cup	button mushrooms, sliced
1	small green bell pepper, roughly chopped	1 cup	raw rice**
1	large onion, roughly chopped and divided	1 ounce	filé powder
		1 teaspoon	fresh thyme, chopped
4	celery stalks, roughly chopped and divided	1	whole bay leaf
			Creole seasoning, to taste
		4	green onions, chopped, for garnish

Before preparing this recipe, prepare the roux according to the instructions on pages 86-87.
* Prepare rice according to directions on pages 90-91.

DIRECTIONS

Preheat the oven to 325°F.

Roast the duck for 45 minutes to an hour until fully cooked. Allow it to cool, pick the meat from it and cut the meat into a large dice. Set meat aside. Reserve the bones and carcass. Pour off fat from roasting pan and reserve for roux. Add olive oil if not enough fat is rendered.

Cook the bones and carcass, the carrot and half of the chopped onion and celery in 2 gallons of water on medium-high heat. Reduce to 1/2 gallon of liquid. Strain and reserve this stock. Add chicken stock if there is not enough liquid.

Make the roux and when it is a peanut butter color add the garlic, peppers and mushrooms, and the remaining half of the onion and celery, adding the Creole seasoning near the end. Add the stock by whisking it in, cup by cup, then bring to a boil.

Add the bay leaf and fresh thyme, reduce heat and allow to simmer. Add the diced duck. Cook for another 20 minutes before seasoning to your taste. Whisk in the filé or serve it on the side to be added in one or two pinches as desired.

Serve over cooked rice with chopped scallions as a colorful garnish.

Mélange is pure entertainment as The Ritz-Carlton's premiere restaurant. When New Orleans' most heralded restaurants share their recipes so The Ritz-Carlton may offer their most famous dishes on one menu, it's a coming together of delicious traditions. As lagniappe, the menu is accented by some of Chef Matt's own culinary creations.

Guests relish a taste of the city and what restaurant wouldn't want to be featured for a Ritz-Carlton guest?

When the landmark Maison Blanche building, a former department store, was revitalized as a grand hotel, it was serendipity that the antique terra cotta exterior was festooned with lion heads, symbol of The Ritz-Carlton.

Chef Gary Darling (right) is the master of the flavor profile. He is also one of the few chefs who had the good fortune to collaborate with the late Chef Warren LeRuth. They devised recipes for Popeyes Fried Chicken that became famous across the country. Gary was yin to Warren's yang in the corporate kitchen.

Gary is intense when it comes to creating new recipes and partnered with Hans Limburg (left) and Greg Reggio (center). The trio named themselves the Taste Buds and created wildly successful restaurants like Semolina, Semolina's Bistro Italia and Zea Rotisserie & Grill.

(Recipe continued)

the buttermilk, coating it completely. Coat each piece again with the flour, coating it completely. Do not shake off the excess flour. Repeat the procedure with all of the chicken pieces.

Heat the oil to 350°F in the large skillet or electric deep fryer. With tongs, add the chicken pieces to the oil, being careful not to have them touching. Fry them to a golden brown, 3 to 5 minutes for small pieces. Remove them with tongs and drain it on newspapers or paper towels.

Add the pieces of fried chicken to the simmering gumbo one at a time. If the chicken has cooled down, continue heating the gumbo until all the chicken pieces are hot. Taste for seasoning and add salt and pepper as desired. Serve in large, shallow soup bowls over cooked white rice.

FRIED CHICKEN GUMBO

This is an excellent way to enjoy an encore fried chicken performance. Otherwise, purchased, prepared chicken fingers are perfectly acceptable, and a time saver. But check the levels of spiciness.

SERVES: 6

1 1/2 cups	vegetable oil	4 quarts	salt-free chicken stock, fresh or canned
2 cups	all-purpose flour	1 sprig	fresh rosemary
1	whole raw chicken, cut into pieces for frying, skin and bones removed	1 teaspoon	dried sage, rubbed
		1 teaspoon	dried thyme
2	large yellow onions, chopped	1/4 teaspoon	cayenne pepper
4	celery stalks, chopped		cooked white rice
3	green bell peppers, chopped		

PREPARING THE GUMBO

In a heavy saucepan, make the roux by heating the oil over medium heat, adding the flour and stirring frequently, until the roux reaches the color of dark-mahogany brown. Be careful not to let it scorch. (Completing the roux will take anywhere from 30 to 45 minutes. Cooking slowly on low heat is the secret to a successful roux.) Add the chopped onions, peppers and celery to the roux. (This will temporarily stop the cooking process.) Cook the roux until the vegetables are tender and translucent, stirring constantly. As the vegetables cook, their sugar will be released and the roux will darken even more as the liquid evaporates.

In a saucepan, warm the chicken stock and add it, cup by cup, to the roux and vegetables in the pot, stirring constantly. Add the rosemary, sage, thyme and cayenne pepper. Simmer, covered, for one hour. While it is simmering, prepare the fried chicken.

TO FRY CHICKEN

2 quarts	peanut oil	1 pound	self-rising flour
2 quarts	whole buttermilk, Bulgarian style preferred		kosher or sea salt, to taste
			black pepper, freshly ground, to taste

Note: *Two pieces of equipment are needed to prepare this recipe—an electric deep-fryer or a deep skillet and a frying thermometer that reads up to 350°F.*

Using two large rectangular or oval roasting pans, each 2 to 3 inches deep, pour the buttermilk into one and the seasoned flour into the other.

The following three-step process results in a full, crunchy coating on the chicken pieces. Coat each piece of chicken with the flour and shake it until only a light dusting of flour remains. Dip each piece into

(Continued on left)

GRIMILLE GUMBO

In the culinary lexicon of south Louisiana, the bits of crumbled meat that join the pan drippings during the roasting of turkey, chicken, ham or beef are called "debris." But the region's Cajuns have always referred to these tasty morsels as grimille (pronounced gree-MEE). By any definition they are too tasty to discard.

If *grimille* is not available, use in its place pieces of a cut-up chicken that have been browned in vegetable oil. When the chicken is almost cooked, remove the pieces from the pan and set them aside to cool. Then remove the skin and bones from the chicken parts and add the meat to the gumbo. Or you can do the same with cubes of chicken breast or turkey meat.

SERVES: 6 to 8

1 cup	vegetable oil		pinch of thyme	
1 cup	all-purpose flour	1/4 cup	parsley, chopped	
2 cups	yellow onion, finely chopped	1 bunch	green onions, chopped	
1 cup	celery, finely chopped	2 1/2 cups	grimille, or browned	
1/3 cup	green bell pepper, finely chopped		chicken	
6 to 8 cups	chicken stock (or more if		pieces, or cubed chicke	
	you prefer a thinner gumbo)		or turkey meat	
	kosher or sea salt and	4 cups	cooked rice	
	cayenne pepper, to taste			

DIRECTIONS

Begin by preparing the roux. Combine the flour and oil in a heavy, 2-quart, cast-iron Dutch oven or deep skillet. Over a medium-low flame, stir the mixture slowly with a whisk (this can take up to 30 or 40 minutes) until the flour begins to turn a rich, golden caramel brown. The process requires almost constant attention. Do not try to multi-task while making roux.

When the flour's color becomes just a shade or two lighter than the caramel brown desired, remove the pot from the burner. The flour will continue to cook in the hot cast-iron pot. While the pot is off the burner, quickly add the chopped onion, celery and bell pepper, stirring to incorporate into the roux. Return the pot to moderate heat and continue stirring until the onion is almost translucent.

Slowly add the chicken stock to the roux, stirring to create a smooth consistency. Add the *grimille*, salt, cayenne pepper and pinch of thyme, and simmer for 1 to 2 hours.

Serve over steamed rice and sprinkle with chopped parsley and green onions.

Marcelle Bienvenu loves the Louisiana bayous and waterways almost as much as its products and cooking them. It is her heritage. She's an all around talented Cajun from St. Martinville, Acadiana's heart and the setting for Longfellow's poem "Evangeline." Marcelle's lovely Cajun accent flavors her comments as much as her garden seasons her creations.

Her family and friends are cooks. Together they're quite a gathering. Marcelle collected the family recipes in a lovely memoir, "Who's Your Mama, Are You Catholic, and Can You Make a Roux?"

She writes a weekly cooking column in The Times-Picayune, New Orleans' daily newspaper. Marcelle is also in great demand as an author and co-author of cookbooks, and has worked with both Emeril Lagasse and Paul Prudhomme, as well as many other nationally noted chefs.

Founded in 1876, P&J Oysters is a New Orleans institution. Most fine restaurants receive their fresh bi-valves daily from the oldest oyster-shucking house in the country, and are glad of it.

The Sunseri family run the operation, as they have always done. That's not unusual in New Orleans, where many customers are also on their third and fourth generation of ownership.

Al Sunseri (left), Merri Sunseri Schneider (center), and Sal Sunseri (right) make certain that oyster lovers have an abundant supply.

OYSTER GUMBO

Oysters are one of the most popular ingredients in New Orleans, with recipes to match. The Sunseri family considers this recipe one of their savory holiday favorites. Who else would know more about oysters than the Sunseri family?

YIELDS: 1 1/2 gallons

1 1/2 cups	flour			black pepper, freshly ground to taste
1 cup	vegetable oil or bacon fat			
3	large onions, medium dice		2	whole bay leaves
1	green bell pepper, medium dice		1/2 cup	parsley, chopped
1 1/2 cups	celery, thin-sliced		1 tablespoon	filé powder
2 quarts	chicken stock, unsalted and preferably fresh			Tabasco sauce, to taste
1 gallon	fresh raw oysters, with juices			cooked rice
	kosher or sea salt, to taste		1 cup	green onions, chopped or chives, chopped, for garnish

DIRECTIONS

Heat a heavy, 8-quart pot and add the oil or bacon fat. When the oil or fat is hot, add the flour and blend the two thoroughly. Using low to moderate heat, cook the roux, stirring and scraping the mixture constantly, until it is the color of peanut butter. This should take between 30 and 45 minutes. During the process, the heat level will need to be adjusted to prevent the flour from scorching.

Add the onion, celery, and green bell pepper to the roux and cook another 15 minutes, stirring constantly, until the onion and celery are translucent.

In a saucepan, warm 2 quarts of the chicken stock and add it, cup by cup, to the roux and vegetables in the pot, stirring constantly until the liquid is incorporated. Simmer, stirring often, until the vegetables almost liquefy, about 1 hour.

Add the oysters and the oyster juices to the stock, along with the salt, pepper and bay leaves, then reduce the heat and simmer 15 minutes.

Remove from heat and sprinkle with parsley and filé powder.

Allow the gumbo to rest for 15 minutes before stirring or serving. Add salt, pepper and Tabasco sauce to taste.

At serving time, if the gumbo has cooled more than desired, return it to the stove and bring it back up to a simmer.

Serve over cooked rice. Garnish with chopped green onions or chives.

QUAIL GUMBO MAMA RACHEL

Chef John Besh, who now owns La Provence following an early-career turn as the sous-chef, says that guests would riot if the late, beloved Chef Chris' quail gumbo was removed from the menu.

SERVES: 6

THE STUFFING

6	semi-boned quail		1/2 cup	smoked sausage, diced
1/4 cup	olive oil		2 cups	cooked rice
1/2	medium onion, chopped fine		6	hard-boiled eggs*, chopped coarsely, for garnish
1 bunch	green onions, chopped			green onions or chives, chopped coarsely for garnish
1/2	medium green bell pepper, chopped fine			
6	sprigs parsley, chopped fine			

*Quail eggs may be difficult to find but hard boiled and halved chicken eggs make a spectacular garnish.

DIRECTIONS

Heat the olive oil in a sauté pan over medium-high heat. When the oil is hot, add the onion, green bell pepper, parsley and smoked sausage and sauté until the onion is translucent. Remove from heat and let cool. Fold the cooked rice in with the sausage and vegetables. Stuff each quail with the rice mixture using 1 tablespoon per quail. Tie the body of each quail, folding the edges toward the middle. Wrap or tightly cover the stuffed quail and temporarily store them in the refrigerator.

THE GUMBO

1 cup	vegetable oil		1 cup	celery. chopped
1 cup	all-purpose flour		2	jalapeño peppers, minced
1 cup	yellow onion, chopped		3 quarts	chicken stock
1 cup	green bell pepper, chopped		2 cups	ripe tomatoes, chopped
1/2 bunch	flat-leaf (Italian) parsley, chopped		2	whole bay leaves
				kosher or sea salt and black pepper, freshly ground, to taste

*Before preparing this recipe, read the instructions for making roux on pages 86-87.

DIRECTIONS

Begin by preparing the roux. Place the vegetable oil in a large, heavy pot and heat the oil just before it reaches the smoking point. Incorporate the flour, a little at a time, into the oil, stirring almost constantly so as not to burn the roux. Cook the roux over low heat, stirring frequently, for about 15 minutes or until the cooked flour reaches a dark brown color. Add the vegetables and continue to cook until the roux becomes a chocolate brown. Add the stock, tomatoes, bay leaves, salt and pepper, and bring the mixture to a boil. *(Continued on right)*

(Recipe continued)

When the boiling point is reached, reduce the heat and allow the gumbo to simmer for about 2 hours, occasionally skimming the impurities from the top. If the gumbo becomes too thick, add more stock. The final liquid should be the consistency of a rich cream soup.

When the gumbo has finished cooking, strain the remaining solids from it, discard the solids, and set the liquid aside.

About an hour before serving, preheat the oven to 425°F.

Once the proper oven temperature is reached, place the reserved quails breast-side-up on a lightly oiled pan. Allow them to cook for 7 to 8 minutes.

To serve, place each stuffed quail breast-side-up in a large, shallow soup or gumbo bowl and add the liquid gently. Top each serving with the chopped equivalent of about 1 hard-cooked egg and 1 green onion.

In the sprawling wetlands and prairies of Cajun country in southwest Louisiana, hunting, fishing and foraging were, at first, the only ways to shop. At times, in the properly licensed seasons, the results are delicacies as well as great sport.

The early Cajuns' diet depended heavily on ducks and venison, trout and bass, shrimp and crabs, and wild berries and herbs from the woods, all of which have always been common in their food-rich world.

Chef John Folse recognizes Louisiana's affinity for game, and consequently published the definitive "After the Hunt: Louisiana's Authoritative Collection of Wild Game & Game Fish Cookery."

JOHN FOLSE

RABBIT, OYSTER AND ANDOUILLE GUMBO

Using smoked meat and seafood in a game soup is quite common in Cajun and Creole cooking, since we are always striving to build flavor. This is a filé gumbo, meaning it contains dried sassafras leaves pounded or ground into a powdery consistency. Gumbo filé, which is a traditional thickener, can be found in most south Louisiana supermarkets and on internet websites.

SERVES: 6

4 cups	raw, boneless rabbit meat, cubed		1/2 cup	green bell pepper, chopped
1 pint	oysters, with liquid		1/4 cup	garlic ,minced
1 pound	andouille sausage, sliced crosswise in pieces about 1/2-inch thick		3 quarts	game stock or water
			2 cups	green onions, sliced
			1/2 cup	parsley, chopped
1 cup	vegetable oil			kosher or sea salt and
1 cup	all-purpose flour			black pepper, freshly cracked, to taste
1 cup	yellow onions, chopped			granulated garlic to taste
1 cup	celery, chopped		1 tablespoon	filé powder

For information on making roux, see pages 86-87.

DIRECTIONS

In a large cast-iron pot, heat the vegetable oil over medium-high heat. Whisk in the flour, stirring constantly, until a dark brown roux* is achieved.

Add onions, celery, bell pepper and minced garlic, and sauté 3 to 5 minutes or until vegetables are wilted.

Add rabbit and andouille pieces and sauté 10 minutes or until browned. Add stock, one ladle at a time, stirring until all is incorporated. Bring to a boil, reduce heat and simmer 1 to 1 1/2 hours or until tender. Add oysters, green onions and parsley.

Season to taste using salt, pepper and granulated garlic. Cook an additional 5 minutes or until oysters begin to curl.

Stir in filé and serve over steamed white rice.

KEVIN VIZARD, VIZARD'S

RIVER PARISHES SEAFOOD GUMBO

This is one of the few gumbo recipes that calls for both okra and filé powder, each a thickener but each also with its own flavor.

SERVES: 8

1 cup	vegetable oil, divided		4 pounds	raw shrimp, shelled
4 cups	onions, chopped		2	whole Louisiana blue crabs, cleaned and halved
1 1/2 cups	celery, chopped		1 cup	parsley, chopped
1/2 cup	bell pepper, chopped		1/2 cup	green onion, chopped
4	garlic cloves, chopped			kosher or sea salt and black pepper, freshly ground, to taste
2 pounds	okra, cut in 1/2 inch slices			
3 tablespoons	all-purpose flour			
4 quarts	shrimp and crab stock*		1 teaspoon	Tabasco sauce
3 large	Creole tomatoes, chopped		1 tablespoon	Worcestershire sauce
1 cup	ham, diced		1 teaspoon	gumbo filé powder
1 teaspoon	dried thyme*		4 cups	cooked rice
1 teaspoon	dried basil			
4	whole bay leaves			

*For a stock recipe see page 85.

**The amounts of thyme, basil and bay leaf for the gumbo should be adjusted according to the corresponding amounts in the crab-and-shrimp stock.

DIRECTIONS

In a large soup pot, sauté the onions, celery, bell pepper and garlic in 1/2 cup of the oil. Watch closely to prevent burning.

Remove 2 tablespoons of the oil from the remaining 1/2 cup and set aside for later use with the roux.

In a skillet, fry the okra in the remaining oil. The okra slices should be cooked for 20 minutes over medium heat to help dry them out a little, so more oil may be needed.

For the roux, heat 2 tablespoons of oil in a skillet over moderate heat. Reduce the heat level to low or medium-low and add the flour, cooking and stirring constantly. Be extremely careful not to burn the roux. When the color of the flour becomes light brown, add the tomatoes to it and cook for 10 minutes. Then add the roux mixture to the soup pot. Add the herbs and ham. After mixing everything in the soup pot, pour the stock into pot. Cook the gumbo at a simmer for 2 hours.

Next, add the shrimp, crabs, okra and remaining seasonings to the pot. Cook for an additional 45 minutes.

Before serving, taste the gumbo for seasoning. Serve over rice and either pass the filé powder at the table or, a couple of minutes before serving, add it to the pot and stir to mix it with the gumbo.

Chef Kevin, a lifelong New Orleanian, is thriving in a cozy, vine-covered building uptown. He likes to cook his way.

He draws on classical flavors, his heritage, and contemporary thinking. This recipe is from his mother and no, he didn't mess with it. It is a marvelous example of a definitive gumbo, darkly rich as a bayou, and loaded with seafood.

Vizard's is a Magazine Street favorite operated with Cammie, his wife, and business partner. Long-time, loyal cooks back him up in the kitchen.

The restaurant is a haven of comfortable food with deep Louisiana roots and Chef Kevin's adept creativity.

New Orleanians dine extravagantly on gumbo and soup, casual concoctions stirred up in local kitchens. Rice is a staple in these dishes; many are served for large gatherings.

It is this kind of Creole pot food cooking that we all enjoy at home. In 1994 Arnaud's Restaurant owner Archie Casbarian converted a building at the end of his properties on Bourbon Street. It is named Remoulade, in honor of Arnaud's sauce and is a café serving a food festival with the best of New Orleans home cooking and fresh seafood. It stands as his nod to casual Creole fare. As lagniappe (a little something extra), Remoulade offers a few of its big sister's specialties such as Oysters Arnaud and Shrimp Arnaud.

The property has a very long history. In 1722, four years after the city's founding, it was identified on the de la Tour map. On January 14, 1795, Don Jorge Inguenberty sold it to Luis Duval, and the transfer of ownership notes, "A house and kitchen exists on this land."

It did then, and it does now.

REMOULADE

Seafood Gumbo

When you get right down to it, there's nothing more New Orleans than a terrific bowl of seafood gumbo.

SERVES: 6 to 8

2 quarts	shrimp or fish stock*	2	whole bay leaves
4	fresh ripe tomatoes, chopped, or a 16-ounce can of tomatoes, drained and chopped	5	Louisiana blue crabs,** cleaned and quartered
4 tablespoons	bacon drippings or olive oil	1	10-ounce package frozen, cut-up okra
4 tablespoons	all-purpose flour	1/2 cup	green onion, finely chopped
1 1/2 cups	celery, finely chopped	1/2 cup	parsley, finely chopped
2 cups	yellow onion, finely chopped	1 teaspoon	black peppercorns, freshly ground, to taste
2 cups	green bell pepper, finely chopped	1/2 teaspoon	cayenne pepper
2	small cloves garlic, minced	2 pounds	raw shrimp, small (40 to 50 per pound) shelled
1 1/2 teaspoons	dried thyme		cooked rice, for serving

* *See page 85 for shrimp-stock recipe.*
** *Preferably, "gumbo crabs," which are hard-shell crabs that are too small or scrawny to be picked for meat lumps.*

DIRECTIONS

Read the instructions for making roux on pages 86-87.

In a stockpot or Dutch oven, combine the shrimp stock and chopped tomatoes and bring to a simmer over medium heat.

Meanwhile, in a heavy saucepan or skillet, prepare the roux. Heat the bacon drippings or olive oil over medium heat. Add the flour and cook, stirring frequently, until the roux reaches the color of café au lait. Be careful not to let it scorch. (This may take anywhere from 30 to 45 minutes.)

Add the celery, yellow onion and green bell pepper and cook for about 10 minutes, stirring frequently until softened. Stir in the garlic and add the thyme and bay leaves. Carefully add the roux mixture to the soup pot. Be careful: The roux tends to spit and pop when it hits the liquid. Cook for 10 minutes over medium heat, stirring occasionally.

Stir in the crab quarters, okra, green onion and parsley, and bring to a boil. Skim off any impurities that may collect on top of the liquid if necessary, then cover the pot and reduce the heat to a simmer.

After 45 minutes stir in the black pepper, cayenne and shrimp. Taste before adding salt. (The salt in the stock and tomatoes may be sufficient.) Cook gently, covered, for about 20 minutes more. Taste and adjust seasonings if necessary before serving over cooked rice.

Seafood Okra Gumbo Classique

Frank Davis is a New Orleans television personality and prolific cookbook author. His quirky take on the city and its characters is pure entertainment, and his knowledge of its best local fishing and cooking is considerable.

Note: *This recipe calls for using a very large pot, with a capacity of at least 10 quarts. Also, before preparing the recipe, read the instructions for making roux on pages 86-87.*

SERVES: 12 to 18

©2008 Mike Sanders

12 tablespoons	vegetable oil, divided
1 pound	smoked sausage, diced
4	16-ounce cans sliced okra or
4	10-ounce packages of sliced frozen okra
2 gallons	water or seafood stock, divided*
2 sticks	corn-oil margarine
6 tablespoons	all-purpose flour
3	large white onions, finely chopped
3 teaspoons	garlic powder
2 tablespoons	liquid crab boil seasoning
3 teaspoons	fresh thyme, chopped
2 pounds	shrimp, shelled and chopped
8	1 1/4-ounce packages of sun-dried shrimp, optional
1 pound	fresh crab meat
12	raw gumbo crabs,** cleaned and quartered
1	16-ounce can tomato sauce
8	whole bay leaves
1/2 cup	parsley, finely chopped
2 tablespoons	kosher or sea salt
3 pounds	shrimp, whole and raw
4 cups	cooked rice

* *See page 85 for a seafood stock recipe.*
** *Hard-shell crabs that are too small or scrawny to be picked for meat lumps.*

DIRECTIONS

Place 6 tablespoons of the vegetable oil in the pot over high heat. Add the smoked sausage and brown well. The fat will be the base for browning the okra. Reduce the heat to medium. Add the okra to the sausage and also brown it well. It should cook in about 20 minutes. Pour in 1 quart of water and let the contents simmer, covered, on low heat.

In a small saucepan, begin preparing a brown roux. Place the remaining 6 tablespoons of vegetable oil, the 2 sticks of margarine and the 6 tablespoons of flour and cook until the flour turns brown. Add the onions, garlic powder, liquid crab boil seasoning and thyme and stir briskly until the onions become tender and translucent. Add the roux mixture to the okra in the large pot and blend together well. Add the remaining 7 quarts of water, increasing the heat level to medium-high and bring to a simmer. Reduce heat to low and allow the liquid to simmer for about 10 minutes, stirring constantly.

Set the whole raw shrimp aside and add the chopped shrimp, sun-dried shrimp (if using), crab meat, gumbo crabs, tomato sauce, seasonings, and stir. The gumbo liquid should be brownish with

(Continued on right)

Frank Davis often notes the importance of advance preparation when making a gumbo. For this one, before the skillet hits the stove the okra should be drained in a colander, the dried shrimp, which are optional, taken from their packets, the crabs cleaned and washed, and the sausage cut.

This will keep you from scrambling while you're preparing your gumbo. In restaurants this is called creating the mise en place. (Think of it as "getting your mess in place.")

In a structured restaurant kitchen, at least one member of the crew collects and readies every ingredient of each dish being prepared. This helps to prevent the cooks from discovering halfway through a recipe that a key ingredient is missing.

(Recipe continued)

a reddish tinge, and the okra should be broken up and suspended in the liquid. Cover the pot and simmer on low heat for about 25 to 30 minutes, stirring occasionally.

Then uncover the pot and add the 3 pounds of whole shrimp. Cook on high heat for about 5 minutes. When the shrimp are done, take the pot off the fire and set it aside, but leave the cover on for 20 more minutes. This will allow the seasonings to blend fully.

Finally, after the gumbo has cooled slightly, toss in the steamed rice and stir it in well. Once again, cover the pot and let the rice grains soften for at least 40 minutes to pick up the flavors. Freeze any leftovers.

Chef Donald Link's German roots are found in the plains country of southwest Louisiana, where his ancestors used their hand-me-down techniques to introduce a wide range of charcuterie to the region. No wonder Link uses a smoker for so many of his meat preparations. His lusty, creative dishes can be found at his two New Orleans restaurants—Cochon, whose menu focuses on country-style treatments of pork, fish and zestily seasoned vegetables, and Herbsaint, a favorite of diners seeking creative and more refined dishes that do not lack for the deep, luscious flavors of the Creole-Cajun style. This extensive repertoire earned Link a James Beard Foundation Award as Best Chef in the Southeast for 2007.

(Recipe continued)

If the gumbo is too thick, add more stock until the consistency you prefer is reached. Using a skillet, fry the bacon until it becomes crisp and brown. Remove bacon, leaving the bacon fat in the skillet. Drain bacon on paper towels. Reheat bacon oil in skillet and add the collard or mustard greens and onions and sauté until wilted. Crumble bacon and return to the greens mixture. Add sugar, vinegar, hot sauce and salt and pepper to taste.

Using a skillet, sear okra in oil until lightly browned. This process helps to remove the stringy consistency that okra can produce. Add the okra, blackeyed peas, greens, pork and seasoning. Return to a simmer and adjust the seasoning to taste. Serve over cooked rice or with a side dish of potato salad.

DONALD LINK, HERBSAINT AND COCHON

SHREDDED PORK GUMBO WITH BLACKEYED PEAS

Seafood and poultry are the most familiar main ingredients of gumbo recipes. This one relies on tender pork and blackeyed peas to underline its deep, smoky flavor. The traditional accompaniment to gumbo is potato salad, so use your favorite recipe for it and serve it as a side dish.

If you have a smoker, prepare your own shredded pork. A raw pork butt, about 2 to 3 pounds, should be coated with Creole seasoning *(See the recipe on page 93.)* and smoked to provide the necessary quantity and flavor. Shred the meat into bite-size pieces. Otherwise, seek out pre-cooked shredded pork, without sauce, from your favorite barbecue restaurant. Blackeyed peas are available in most good markets, fresh and ready to cook. The dried peas must be soaked and then cooked for the appropriate amount of time. It would be tempting to use a canned product, well seasoned.

SERVES: 6

1 1/2 cups	all-purpose flour	2 cups cooked	blackeyed peas, or substitute one 15-1/2-ounce can
1 cup	vegetable oil or bacon grease	1 1/2 pounds	pulled, shredded pork, fully smoked
2 cups	yellow onion, finely diced	2 tablespoons	filé powder
1 cup	green pepper, finely diced	1 tablespoon	fresh thyme, chopped
1/2 cup	celery, finely diced	1 tablespoon	chile powder
3 tablespoons	garlic, finely chopped	1 tablespoon	paprika
1 1/2 gallons	pork or chicken stock,* unsalted and preferably fresh	1 tablespoon	white pepper
		2 tablespoons	black pepper
1 1/2 pounds	fresh okra sliced crosswise 1/2 inch wide	1 tablespoon	cayenne pepper
2 tablespoons	vegetable oil for okra	3	whole bay leaves

FOR GREENS

2 cups	cooked collard or mustard greens	1 tablespoon	granulated sugar
4 pieces	bacon, fried	1 teaspoon	white vinegar
1	white onion, finely chopped		hot sauce to taste

See page 85 for chicken stock recipe.

DIRECTIONS

Prepare a dark-mahogany-colored roux using the flour and oil *(See pages 86-87)*. Stir continuously and pay close attention as the color darkens. Preparation will require 30 to 45 minutes. As soon as the roux is just past a red color and turning back to brown, add the diced vegetables and chopped garlic. Add the stock and, stirring frequently, bring to a simmer. Continue simmering for about 1 hour while frequently stirring. Skim off all of the fat that rises to the top. *(Continued on left)*

JOHN FOLSE

SMOKED WOOD DUCK AND ANDOUILLE GUMBO

Almost every species of wild game in Louisiana has been used in the creation of gumbo. Because Cajun men historically have been farmers, hunters and trappers, it is not surprising that wild duck and andouille sausage were often used in home kitchens. The wood duck, which inhabits wooded swamps and streams, is one of the few North American ducks that nest in trees.

SERVES: 6

3	smoked wood ducks, halved	1/2 cup	yellow bell pepper, chopped
1 pound	andouille sausage, sliced crosswise in pieces about 1/2 inch thick	1/4 cup	garlic, minced
			kosher or sea salt and black pepper, freshly ground, to taste
1 gallon	cold water		granulated garlic to taste
1 cup	vegetable oil		Creole seasoning to taste
1 1/4 cups	all-purpose flour		Louisiana hot sauce to taste
2 cups	yellow onion, chopped	2 cups	green onions, sliced
2 cups	celery, chopped	1 cup	parsley, chopped
1/2 cup	green bell pepper, chopped	2 tablespoons	filé powder
1/2 cup	red bell pepper, chopped		cooked rice

*For information on making roux, see pages 86-87.

DIRECTIONS

Filé is dried sassafras leaves pounded or ground into a powdery consistency. Gumbo filé, which is a traditional thickener, can be found in most south Louisiana supermarkets and on internet websites.

Smoke the wood ducks in a home-style smoker according to manufacturer's directions. It is not necessary to smoke ducks beyond rare since the flavor of smoke rather than the cooking temperature is most important to this recipe.

In a 2-gallon stockpot over medium-high heat, combine duck halves, andouille and water. Bring to a rolling boil, then reduce to simmer and cook until wood ducks are tender, 30 to 45 minutes.

Remove ducks and andouille from the pot and reserve 3 quarts of stock. When ducks have cooled, bone and set them aside.

In a large Dutch oven, heat vegetable oil over medium-high heat. Add flour and, using a wire whisk, stir constantly until a dark brown roux* is achieved. Add onion, celery, bell pepper and minced garlic. Sauté 3 to 5 minutes or until vegetables are wilted. Add duck and andouille, blending well into the vegetable mixture. Add reserved stock, one ladle at a time, stirring constantly, until a soup-like consistency is achieved. Bring mixture to a rolling boil, then reduce to simmer and cook 45 minutes. During the cooking process, season the gumbo at 20-minute intervals, using salt, pepper, granulated garlic, Creole seasoning and hot sauce. Add green onions, parsley and filé powder and blend well into gumbo. Cook an additional 5 minutes. Serve gumbo over steamed white rice.

Louisiana isn't called a Sportsman's Paradise for nothing. Like so many of the state's natives, Chef John Folse is an avid hunter who is passionate about wild game and always cooks what he hunts. He's written several cookbooks, the most recent being "After the Hunt: Louisiana's Authoritative Collection of Wild Game & Game Fish Cookery." An earlier work was "The Encyclopedia of Cajun and Creole Cuisine," a labor of love about the state's culinary history.

There's not much Folse doesn't do for Louisiana's culinary community. For example, he was the driving force behind the establishment of the John Folse Culinary Institute at Nicholls State University.

CHRISTOPHER GROMEK

TULANE CHICKEN ANDOUILLE GUMBO

This gumbo recipe is among the relatively few that use no roux.

SERVES: 6 to 8

1	whole raw chicken, weighing about 3 pounds	1 quart	water
2 tablespoons	vegetable oil	1	large white onion, minced
1 tablespoon	Tony Chachere's Creole Seasoning, or the Creole seasoning recipe on page 93	1	medium green bell pepper, minced
1 pound	andouille sausage, sliced into 1/4-inch rounds	3	celery stalks, minced
		2	whole bay leaves
2	10-ounce packages frozen okra, sliced	4	garlic cloves, minced
			gumbo filé powder, to taste
2 quarts	fresh chicken stock*	4 cups	cooked white rice

See page 85 for a chicken stock recipe.

DIRECTIONS

Cut the chicken into pieces and set aside the back, gizzards, and liver to make the chicken stock. Lightly dust the chicken pieces with the Creole seasoning.

Using a skillet large enough to hold all the pieces without crowding, brown the chicken in the vegetable oil over medium heat. Turn the chicken pieces with tongs every few minutes to brown them evenly. After the chicken pieces have browned, remove and set them aside to cool. Using the same skillet, brown the andouille slices and set aside.

Add the okra slices to the skillet and also brown them well. If there is not enough remaining vegetable oil in which to brown the okra, add a tablespoon of the oil to the skillet. Since frozen okra is not nearly as sticky and stringy as fresh okra, it should cook well in about 20 minutes. When the okra is cooked, pour in the 1 quart of water and let the contents simmer, covered, on low heat.

Pour 2 quarts of the chicken stock into a 4-quart Dutch oven or another heavy pot. Add the onion, bell pepper, celery, bay leaves and garlic. Next, add the okra with the water and increase the heat level to bring the liquid to a rolling boil. When that boiling point is reached, reduce the heat level to moderate. Cover the pot and allow to simmer for 1/2 hour. Then add the chicken and sausage and simmer another 1/2 hour. After the gumbo has finished cooking, discard the bay leaves.

At serving time, ladle the gumbo into the bowls over cooked rice. Pass the filé powder in a small bowl. Most fans of filé gumbo usually sprinkle a fairly generous pinch of the powder over the gumbo.

Christopher came to our test kitchen as a summer assistant from Tulane University, and never left. He was able to take the leftovers, and living in a house shared by other students, he became the go-to guy on campus for food, and lots of it.

His guests believe he is a culinary wizard. Not a bad reputation.

Novice cooks testing recipes are wonderful, because lack of clarity, omissions, or mistakes become obvious.

Quickly, for a young man who couldn't cook, he got into the groove, wielding a knife, and stirring roux. Christopher has learned how and where to shop, and to eyeball fresh seafood. He also developed quite a palate and can discuss the variations of gumbo with authority.

He's one more convert, able to spread the tastes of New Orleans cooking that will travel wherever he lands.

TURKEY AND ANDOUILLE GUMBO

Gumbo is one of those exemplary dishes that can be made in any number of ways. The emphasis is on the main ingredients: meats, poultry, seafood or almost any combination of them. Roux and the trinity of seasonings create a smoky, dense taste, rich in texture and full of flavor. In south Louisiana, families get together for holidays and cook up a continuous two- or three-day food fest beginning with visits to the farmers' markets and grocery stores. Messing around with Mama's recipe will get almost anyone in trouble.

YIELD: 2 gallons   SERVES: 16 to 20

1	whole turkey carcass	2 tablespoons	garlic, minced
3 cups	all-purpose flour	1 1/2 gallons	chicken and turkey broth, homemade or canned. (This should include the liquid in which the turkey carcass was cooked.)
2 cups	corn oil, to make roux		
2 large	yellow onions, chopped		
3	green bell peppers, chopped		
4	celery stalks, chopped		
2 cans	your favorite local beer or an equal amount of stock or water	1 tablespoon	dried basil
		1 tablespoon	dried oregano
3 tablespoons	Worcestershire sauce	1 tablespoon	dried thyme
1/4 cup	Tabasco or Crystal hot sauce	1/4 teaspoon	cayenne pepper
1 tablespoon	corn oil, to sauté sausage		cooked rice, for serving
1 pound	andouille or Hillshire Farms smoked sausage, thinly sliced, cut crosswise into half-moons		

Before preparing this recipe, read the instructions for making roux on pages 86-87.

DIRECTIONS

Cut the turkey carcass in half and, in a large pot, simmer the halves in water to cover until the remaining meat falls off the bones.

Drain and reserve the cooking water. Remove the meat from the bones and discard the bones. Shred the meat. (If this does not yield 2 to 3 cups of turkey, add any poultry meat.)

In a heavy saucepan, make the roux by heating the 2 cups of corn oil over medium heat, adding the flour and cooking, stirring frequently, until the roux reaches the color of milk chocolate. Be careful not to let it scorch. (Completing the roux will take anywhere from 30 to 45 minutes. Cooking slowly on low heat is the secret to succeeding with roux.)

Add the chopped onions, peppers and celery to the roux. (This will temporarily stop the cooking process.) Cook the roux until the vegetables are tender, stirring constantly. As the vegetables cook, their sugar will be released and the roux will darken even more as the liquid evaporates. Stir in the beer (or stock or water), the Worcestershire and the hot sauce. *(Continued on right)*

© 2008 Photograph Frankie Frankeny

My nephew Robert Barker's cooking career started with potato-peeling duty as a youngster. Later, his skills were honed in New Orleans at Delgado Community College's Culinary Arts Apprenticeship Program. Every year at Thanksgiving he returns to the city to put those skills to glorious use in my kitchen, supervising the preparation of a multi-course feast. Afterward, Robert makes a stock with the turkey carcasses. Then we feast again, on turkey and andouille gumbo.

(Recipe continued)

In a large Dutch oven or the original soup pot, sauté the sausage and garlic in one tablespoon of oil until the garlic is translucent and soft. Carefully add the roux mixture to the pot, stirring. (It will spit and sputter.)

Add the turkey broth and stir in the basil, oregano, thyme and cayenne pepper. I've seen Chef Robert add the leftover turkey gravy to the gumbo. Simmer, covered, for one hour, then add the shredded turkey and cook for 20 minutes more. Taste for seasoning and add more salt and pepper as desired.

Serve in bowls over cooked rice.

© Photograph Michael Terranova

Mr. B's stands for Brennan's, another mighty offshoot of the restaurant group – the Commander's Palace side of the family, if you're keeping score. Managing Partner Cindy Brennan works closely with Executive Chef Michelle McRaney to provide Creole-style specialties in the French Quarter.

GUMBO YA-YA

Legend says that the term "gumbo ya-ya" was a French-based dialect spoken in New Orleans during the 1800s. The late New Orleans author Lyle Saxon borrowed it for the title of his book of Louisiana folk tales. Another school of thought says that "gumbo ya-ya" referred to the chattering of women while they cooked in 19th century New Orleans. Cindy Brennan, proprietor of Mister B's Bistro in the French Quarter, says the restaurant's gumbo ya-ya is the best-selling dish on the menu.

YIELD: about 6 quarts

1 pound (4 sticks)	unsalted butter	1 teaspoon	black pepper, freshly ground
3 cups	all-purpose flour	1 teaspoon	dried hot red-pepper flakes
2	red bell peppers, diced		
2	green bell peppers, diced	1 teaspoon	chile powder
2	medium onions, diced	1 teaspoon	dried thyme
2	celery stalks, diced	1 tablespoon	garlic, minced
1 1/4 gallons (20 cups)	chicken stock	2	whole bay leaves
1 pound	andouille sausage, cut into 1/4-inch-thick slices	1	3-1/2-pound chicken, roasted and boned
2 tablespoons	Creole seasoning		hot sauce to taste
2 tablespoons	kosher or sea salt plus additional to taste		boiled or steamed rice

Andouille is a lean and spicy pork sausage made in south Louisiana. Any good-quality pork sausage, such as kielbasa, may be substituted.

DIRECTIONS

Begin by making a dark roux.* In a 12-quart stockpot melt the butter over low heat. Gradually add 1 cup of the flour, stirring constantly with a wooden spoon, and continue cooking, stirring constantly, for 30 seconds. Add 1 more cup of flour and stir constantly for 30 seconds. Add the remaining cup flour and stir constantly for 30 seconds. Continue to cook the roux, stirring constantly, until it is the color of dark mahogany, about 45 minutes to 1 hour.

Add the red and green bell peppers to the roux and stir constantly for 30 seconds. Add the onions and celery and stir constantly for 30 seconds. Gradually add stock to the roux, stirring constantly with a wooden spoon to prevent lumps. Add the andouille sausage, Creole seasoning, salt, black pepper, red pepper flakes, chile powder, thyme, garlic and bay leaves, and bring to a boil. Simmer gumbo, uncovered, for 45 minutes, skimming off any fat and stirring occasionally.

Add chicken meat and simmer 15 minutes. Adjust seasoning with salt and hot sauce.

Serve over rice.

For information on making roux, see pages 86-87.

LEAH CHASE, DOOKIE CHASE'S
GUMBO Z'HERBES

Gumbo z'herbes (or, literally speaking, gumbo aux herbes) was, for Creole Catholics, a dish traditionally eaten on Holy Thursday, three days before Easter. The custom lives on in chef Leah Chase's kitchen at her restaurant, Dooky Chase's, where a tradition-minded crowd gathers every year. This gumbo recipe is one of the few that do not call for a roux. The ingredients include meat, but an equally authentic version is made with greens only.

SERVES: 8

1 bunch	mustard greens			water
1 bunch	collard greens		1 pound	chaurice*
1 bunch	turnip greens		1 pound	smoked ham
1 bunch	watercress		1 pound	brisket stew meat
1 bunch	beet tops		1 pound	boneless brisket
1 bunch	carrot tops		1 pound	hot pork sausage*
1/2 head	lettuce		5 teaspoons	all-purpose flour
1/2 head	cabbage		1 teaspoon	fresh thyme leaves
1 bunch	spinach		1 tablespoon	kosher or sea salt
2	medium onions, chopped		1 teaspoon	cayenne pepper
4	garlic cloves, chopped and mashed		1 teaspoon	filé powder
				steamed rice

*Chaurice is a peppery Cajun pork sausage. Any good-quality pork sausage, such as kielbasa, may be substituted.

DIRECTIONS

Clean all the greens under cold water to remove grit. Pick out all bad leaves and discard. With a knife, or by hand, shred all the greens into rough 1/2-inch pieces. Put all greens, onions, and garlic in an 8-quart stockpot, cover with water, and boil over high heat for 30 minutes. While the vegetables are boiling, cut all meats into bite-size pieces, and set aside, keeping the pieces of sausage separate.

After boiling for 30 minutes, remove the pot from heat and strain the vegetables out of the liquid, but retain the broth. In a 12-quart stockpot, place all meats—except the sausage—and 2 cups of the reserved broth. Cook the meats with the broth over high heat for 15 minutes. While the meats are cooking, place the sausage pieces in a skillet over high heat and sauté until all fat is rendered, about 10 minutes. Remove them from the skillet and retain the rendered fat.

In a food processor, purée all vegetables. Reheat the fat rendered from the sausage over high heat. Gradually stir the flour into the fat to create a white roux,* cooking the mixture and stirring constantly for 5 minutes, or until the flour and fat are well combined. Pour the roux over the meat mixture in the large stockpot and stir well. Add the vegetables to the large stockpot, along with 2 quarts of the reserved broth. Place the stockpot over a low flame, and allow to simmer for 20 minutes. Add the sausage, thyme, salt and cayenne, and stir well. Simmer for 40 minutes over low heat. Add filé powder, stir well once again and remove from heat. Serve over steamed white rice.

*For information on making roux, see pages 86-87.

In New Orleans, Leah Chase holds the undisputed title of Queen of Creole Cuisine. Her realm is headquartered at Dooky Chase's, where such luminaries as Martin Luther King Jr., composer Duke Ellington, Supreme Court Justice Thurgood Marshall, author James Baldwin and singer Ray Charles regularly stopped by for her blue-ribbon versions of jambalaya, fried chicken, red beans and rice and a long list of other Creole classics. She also has hosted two presidents of the United States in the restaurant's dining rooms, where the display showcases prints and paintings by some of America's most respected artists, including a good many New Orleanians.

Leah also has made personal appearances all over the country, delivering the message that Creole cooking remains unequaled among America's regional cuisines.

| 45

Lüke is Chef John Besh's version of an old New Orleans brasserie from the turn of the past century.

The menu's mainstays are fresh seafood, charcuterie and hearty dishes combining French and German Old World cooking.

Lüke's decor includes rattan bistro chairs, blackboard specials and newspaper racks. Focal points such as tin ceilings, an oyster bar and a glassed-in kitchen create a warm and casual ambiance.

An acclaimed chef and Louisiana native, John Besh also presides over Restaurant August, Besh Steak and La Provence.

JOHN BESH, LÜKE

CRAB AND CORN BISQUE

A heart-warming bisque that deserves the freshest ingredients to meld compatible, subtle flavors.

SERVES: 10 to 12

2 tablespoons	olive oil	2 tablespoons	unsalted butter
1 pound	gumbo crabs*	4	ears of fresh corn
1	onion, chopped	1 pound	jumbo lump crab meat, picked
1	celery stalk, chopped		clean of shells, Louisiana blue
3	garlic cloves		crabs preferred
1 1/2 cups	heavy cream		kosher or sea salt, to taste
1	fresh thyme sprig		freshly ground black pepper,
1	whole bay leaf		to taste
1 cup	raw rice		Tabasco sauce, to taste
1 tablespoon	tomato paste		

*Hard-shell crabs that are too small or scrawny to be picked for meat lumps.

DIRECTIONS

With a serrated knife, remove the corn kernels from the cob and set aside.

Place the corn cobs in a pot of water, to cover. Over medium heat, bring the corn stock to a simmer. When the stock has simmered for 1 hour, remove the cobs from the stock and discard them. Reserve the stock.

Heat the olive oil in a large pot over medium heat for 2 minutes. Add the crabs to the oil and sauté them for another 10 minutes. Then add the onion, garlic and celery and sweat together for an additional 5 minutes. Add the tomato paste at this point and sauté for 2 more minutes.

Add the stock and bring it to a boil. Add the rice, thyme, bay leave and heavy cream. Allow the mixture to simmer for 30 minutes. Purée the soup in the blender and strain with a fine-meshed sieve. Sauté the corn and crab meat in the butter until hot and add it to the soup.

Season with salt, pepper and Tabasco sauce to taste.

MARCELLE BIENVENU

CRAWFISH BISQUE

Marcelle Bienvenu loves the south Louisiana bayous and waterways almost as much as her passion for its products and cooking them. It is her heritage. She's an all around talented Cajun from St. Martinville, Acadiana's heart. Her accent flavors her comments as much as her garden seasons her creations. There's no one most appropriate to prepare and serve crawfish bisque than Marcelle. She's been the go to lady for famous chefs, including Emeril Lagasse, Paul Prudhomme, and worked with Ella Brennan at Commander's Palace even before Paul cooked there. She's an author, commentator, and columnist.

Crawfish bisque is the epitome of crustacean fascination. A silky smooth base laced with fresh crawfish tails and vegetables brings into play all of the Creole and Cajun culinary skills. The glory of a great bisque is the stuffing, encased in the crawfish shell heads. It is not really the head, but the shoulder's shell, so don't wince. A savory stuffing of crawfish, bread, crawfish fat, and seasonings packed into it is prepared and placed into the bisque as a little lagniappe, an extra treat.

Should shells not be available, little balls, or boulettes, of the crawfish stuffing, about a tablespoon, can be placed in the oven to brown and serve the same purpose to float in the bisque or as an hors d'oeuvre. This is the queen of Creole recipes so plan to take your time and enjoy the preparation with a friend or two to help and laugh together.

SERVES: 10 to 12

BISQUE

1 cup	vegetable oil or butter		4 medium	onions, chopped
2 1/2 pounds	crawfish tails, peeled		4 medium	green bell peppers, seeded and chopped
1 cup	crawfish fat (or 1/2 cup butter)		4 ribs	celery, chopped
2 tablespoons	kosher or sea salt		6 to 8 cups	tepid water
1 tablespoon	cayenne pepper		2 tablespoons	green onions, chopped
2 tablespoons	paprika		2 tablespoons	fresh parsley, chopped
1 1/2 cups	hot water		5 to 8 cups	cooked white rice
4 tablespoons	dark brown roux			

DIRECTIONS

Heat 1/2 cup of the oil in a large, heavy pot or Dutch oven over medium heat. Add the crawfish tails, crawfish fat or butter, salt, cayenne, and paprika. Cook, stirring for 3 minutes. Combine the water and the roux in a small pot over medium heat and stir to blend. Add to the crawfish mixture, cook for 2 minutes, stirring occasionally.

Meanwhile, in another large pot, heat the remaining 1/2 cup oil over medium heat. Add the onions, bell peppers, and celery. Sauté until soft and golden, about 8 minutes. Remove from the heat and add the vegetables to the crawfish mixture. Add 3 to 4 cups of water, stirring to blend. Cook until the mixture thickens, about 2 minutes, stirring occasionally. Reduce the heat to medium-low and add the remaining water. Cook until the bisque is slightly thick, about 15 minutes. It should be the consistency of a thick soup. Add the stuffed crawfish heads, the green onions, and the parsley. Cook for about 5 minutes, stirring gently. Serve over steamed white rice.

STUFFING

1 cup	vegetable oil or butter
3 medium	onions, minced
4 ribs	celery, chopped
4 medium	green bell peppers, seeded, and minced
5 cloves	fresh garlic, minced
1/2 cup	crawfish fat (if available, If not use 1/2 cup butter)
1 1/2 pounds	crawfish tails, peeled
8 to 10 sliced	day-old bread, soaked In water and squeezed dry
2 tablespoons	kosher or sea salt
1 tablespoon	freshly ground black pepper
1 tablespoon	cayenne pepper
150	crawfish heads, cleaned
1 cup	unseasoned bread crumbs
1 cup	seasoned bread crumbs

DIRECTIONS

Heat 1/2 cup of the oil or butter in a large, heavy pot over medium heat. Add the onions, celery, bell peppers and garlic. Sauté the vegetables until they are soft and golden, 8 to 10 minutes. Add the crawfish fat or butter and cook, stirring for 3 minutes. Remove from the heat and set aside. Grind 1 pound of the crawfish tails and the bread together in a meat grinder or food processor.

Heat the remaining 1/2 cup oil (or butter) in a large, heavy pot or Dutch oven over medium heat. Add the crawfish/bread mixture, the cooked vegetables, salt, black pepper, cayenne, and the remaining 1/2 pound of crawfish tails. Cook, stirring, for 5 to 8 minutes. Remove from the heat and cool to room temperature, stirring it several times as it cools. Combine the bread crumbs together in a small bowl and set aside. Preheat the oven to 375°F.

Stuff each crawfish head with about 1 tablespoon of the stuffing mixture and place on a large baking sheet. Cover the stuffing in the crawfish heads with a generous amount of the bread crumbs, patting it gently to adhere to the stuffing. Bake until the bread crumbs are lightly golden brown, 15-20 minutes. Remove from the oven and set aside.

Oysters stewed in cream is a dish as rich as the history of Arnaud's, which first opened in 1918. When the dish makes an appearance in the dining room, it is as much a star as the pinpoints of light from crystal chandeliers dancing along an equally glittery wall of etched and beveled glass.

The restaurant began as a family establishment, headed by Arnaud Cazenave, who liked to be called "the count," even though the title had no official connection. In 1978 Archie and Jane Casbarian took a leap of faith and purchased Arnaud's, and then restored the legendary grande dame to its original splendor. Since then, the couple's children, Archie Jr. and Katy, have joined the restaurant's management. The next generation of Casbarians began arriving in 2008 with the birth of Archie Alexander Casbarian.

The restaurant encompasses 13 historic structures, with the original Italian mosaic-tile floor patterns changing from one building to the other.

THE CASBARIAN FAMILY, ARNAUD'S

Oysters Stewed in Cream

Those of us who live in New Orleans count oyster soup, with fresh Louisiana oysters poached in simple broth of milk, cream, butter and aromatic seasonings, as one of our blessings. The soup's brightness and clarity of flavor showcases the best of the region's shellfish.

SERVES: 4 to 6

3 1/2 cups	water	1/8 teaspoon	ground red pepper
2 dozen	raw oysters, freshly shucked and drained	1	whole bay leaf
1/2 cup	yellow onion, chopped	3/4 cup	heavy cream
1/2 cup	celery, chopped	2 cups	whole milk
1/2 cup	green onions, chopped	1/2 cup	all-purpose flour
1 tablespoon plus 1/4 cup	unsalted butter	1 teaspoon	kosher or sea salt
1/2 teaspoon	garlic, minced	1/4 teaspoon	white peppercorns, freshly ground
1/8 teaspoon	dried thyme		

DIRECTIONS

In a medium-size saucepan bring the water to a boil. Add oysters and continue to boil for 3 minutes, until the edges curl.

Remove the oysters with a slotted spoon and reserve 3 cups of the liquid. Set both aside.

In a Dutch oven over medium heat, cook the celery, onion and green onions in 1 tablespoon of the butter, stirring constantly until tender. Stir in 2 1/2 cups of the reserved liquid, and the garlic, thyme, red pepper and bay leaf. Bring to a boil, then stir in the cream. Reduce the heat and simmer for 5 minutes. Stir in the milk and return to a simmer. Set aside.

Melt the remaining 1/4 cup butter in a small saucepan over low heat. Add the flour, stirring with a wire whisk until smooth. Cook 4 minutes, stirring constantly, or until smooth. (The mixture will be very thick.)

Gradually add the flour mixture to the milk mixture, stirring until they are blended. Add the oysters, salt and white pepper. Heat the soup thoroughly.

Remove from the heat, discard bay leaf and serve immediately.

JOHN BESH, RESTAURANT AUGUST

REDFISH COURTBOUILLON

Redfish courtbouillon has been a favorite of Creole cooks for well over a century. As used in New Orleans, the word "courtbouillon" differs somewhat in meaning from the original French term, which refers to a poaching liquid, usually water seasoned with vegetables, spices and white wine.

SERVES: 12

COURTBOULLION

3	onions, medium diced		1 gallon	seafood stock
2	green bell peppers, medium diced		2 cups	blond roux*
			1 bunch	fresh tarragon, roughly chopped
1/2 head	celery, medium diced		1 bunch	fresh basil, roughly chopped
4	garlic cloves, minced			kosher or sea salt, to taste
1/2 cup	canola oil			cayenne pepper, to taste
10 pounds	Creole tomatoes, chopped		1/4 teaspoon	allspice, grated

See pages 86-87 for a roux recipe.

DIRECTIONS

Pour the canola oil into a 5-quart Dutch oven or stockpot over medium heat and sauté the onions, green bell peppers, garlic and celery until they are soft and the onions are transparent.

Season the vegetables to taste with salt and cayenne pepper, then add the seafood stock. Bring the liquid to a simmer and mix in the blond roux. Cook for 10 minutes over medium heat. Add the Creole tomatoes, basil, tarragon and allspice, and set aside.

SEAFOOD

1/4 cup	Creole seasoning*		1 quart	shucked raw oysters with liquor, Louisiana oysters preferred
1 head	fresh garlic, chopped			
12	redfish fillets, trimmed to 4-ounce servings		1 1/2 pounds	cooked jumbo lump crabmeat, Louisiana blue crabs preferred, divided into 12 equal portions
24	whole raw medium shrimp to large size, shelled			green onions, chopped to garnish
1 cup	olive oil			

See pages 86-87 for a Creole seasoning recipe.

DIRECTIONS

Preheat the oven to 400°F. Mix the olive oil, Creole seasoning and garlic in a bowl. Add the shrimp and redfish and toss them until they are coated with the oil.

Sear the shrimp and redfish in batches in a cast-iron skillet just until they are rare. Place 1 redfish fillet and 2 shrimp into 8 to 12 ounce individual casserole dishes and fill each dish with 8 ounces of the courtbouillon. *(Continued on right)*

Photograph Will Crocker

A lifelong fisherman and hunter, John Besh is as much at home in the fertile marshes, woods and swamps of southeast Louisiana as he is in the kitchen at any of his four restaurants. The grand and glorious Restaurant August offers Besh's celebrated signature dishes in grand, yet inviting, surroundings. Lüke is a recreation of the classic French brasserie in both its menu and décor. La Provence celebrates Louisiana's French origins with the kind of food and environment found in the south of France. And Besh Steak yields to no other restaurant in the city when it comes to two-fisted slabs of beef. The long list of awards John has won includes that of Best Chef in the Southeast from the James Beard Foundation.

(Recipe continued)

Bake the seafood courtbouillon servings for 10 minutes at 400°F.

Remove them and add six oysters and the jumbo lump crab meat and 6 oysters to each serving and bake for an additional 2 minutes. Top with chopped fresh green onions and serve with rice.

SHRIMP BISQUE

Other recipes for shrimp bisque are simpler and quicker to prepare. But for authentic, rich flavor, this one is worth the extra steps.

SERVES: 6 to 8

1 1/2 pounds	fresh raw medium shrimp (30 to 35 per pound) with heads	2	garlic cloves, finely chopped
2 quarts	shrimp stock*	1/2 teaspoon	fresh thyme leaves, chopped
2 large	fresh ripe tomatoes, chopped	4 tablespoons	tomato purée
1/2 cup	unsalted butter	1/4 cup	brandy plus
1 cup	yellow onion, finely chopped	1/8 cup	brandy for garnish
		3/4 cup	raw, long-grain white rice
2	leeks, white part only, finely chopped	1/2 teaspoon	white peppercorns, freshly ground
2 tablespoons	French shallots, finely chopped		kosher or sea salt to taste
		1 teaspoon	olive oil
		1 tablespoon	fresh parsley, chopped for garnish

*See page 85 for shrimp-stock recipe.

DIRECTIONS

Place 1 quart of the shrimp stock in a large pot with the chopped tomatoes and simmer for 30 minutes.

In the meantime, melt the butter in a medium saucepan and sauté the chopped onion and leek until the onion is translucent. Add the chopped shallot, garlic and thyme and sauté 5 minutes more. Add the tomato purée and cook until browned, stirring often to prevent scorching.

Warm the brandy in a small saucepan and add it to the pan to deglaze. Carefully ignite the mixture in the sauce pan with a long match or fireplace lighter.

After the flames subside add the shrimp, reserving 1 for each bowl as garnish, white pepper, rice and remaining 1 quart of stock. Stir well and simmer for about 30 minutes, until the rice is cooked.

Purée the mixture in batches, using a food processor or blender. Adjust the seasoning, adding salt if necessary.

Strain the bisque back into the saucepan by pushing it through a sieve or strainer. If you desire especially smooth bisque, strain it twice. Simmer over low heat another 20 minutes. Quickly sauté the shrimp for garnish in a small skillet using a teaspoon of olive oil. Set aside.

Serve in shallow gumbo bowls or demitasse cups. Garnish with a shrimp, parsley and a small splash of brandy if desired.

Arnaud's Chef Tommy DiGiovanni is the keeper of the restaurant's shrimp bisque recipe, so this one comes compliments of Chef Tommy as the dish is served at Arnaud's. Tommy has cooked for celebrities, heads of state, royalty and presidents.

A native New Orleanian, he has spent most of his life in a kitchen and his food represents classic Creole, French and Italian cooking.

As sous-chef, he left Arnaud's to gain even more experience. Tommy then returned as executive chef. A banner stretched across the kitchen was emblazoned "Welcome Home, Tommy. He has been home now for a long time.

MICHAEL SHINDLE

Shrimp, Tomato and Corn Bisque

When shrimp, tomatoes and corn are all in season, we celebrate by cooking them in dozens of different ways. That's why Michael's shrimp, corn and tomato bisque is best at that time. If you can't wait for the seasons to converge, you can fake it with canned and frozen products; the bisque is still a treat. It can serve as an elegant first course in demitasses or as a hearty main dish in large bowls.

SERVES: 8 as a main course or 16 as an appetizer

1/2 teaspoon	cayenne pepper	1/2 cup	all-purpose flour
1 teaspoon	black pepper, freshly ground	1 cup	onion, chopped
1 1/2 cups	small cooked shrimp, shelled	1 cup	celery, minced
1 cup	whole milk	1 cup	green bell pepper, chopped
1 cup	heavy cream	1 quart	fresh or canned low-sodium
1/4 cup	flat-leaf (Italian) parsley,		chicken, fish or shrimp stock*
	chopped for garnish, optional	2 cups	fresh or frozen corn kernels
1/4 cup	green onion, chopped	2	tomatoes, skinned, seeded,
	for garnish, optional		crushed and chopped
	sprigs of fresh thyme,	2 teaspoons	dried thyme
	for garnish, optional	1 teaspoon	kosher or sea salt to taste
6 tablespoons	unsalted butter		

See page 85 for stock recipes.

DIRECTIONS

First, begin making a tan-colored "blond" roux by melting the butter in a large, heavy saucepan or Dutch oven over medium heat. Stir in the flour and cook, continue stirring often. Meanwhile, adjust the heat, being careful not to burn the flour, until the roux's color begins to reach the light tan stage. Add the onion, celery and bell pepper. Stir and cook until the onion and celery are almost translucent and the flour is a tan color.

Heat the stock and add it gradually to the roux mixture, whisking until smooth. Bring the liquid to a simmer, adjusting the heat as necessary. Add the corn, chopped tomatoes, thyme, salt, cayenne and black pepper and allow the mixture to simmer for 5 to 6 minutes.

Add the shrimp and stir in the milk and heavy cream. Return the liquid to a simmer. Once you have added the milk and cream, keep the bisque below the boiling point to prevent curdling.

When the bisque is ready to serve, reheat and ladle it into warmed soup bowls or demitasses.

Garnish each with chopped parsley and green onions or with sprigs of fresh thyme.

Michael Shindle has a love affair with New Orleans. He was cooking in the city in August 2005, when Hurricane Katrina struck, and simply took a job elsewhere. When the city's restaurants began reopening he was back almost before someone could say, "The power's back on."

More recently, Michael has been working his way through the positions in the "brigade," the traditional hierarchy of a restaurant kitchen's staff. The progression can lead to such top positions as sous-chef, chef de cuisine and, ultimately, executive chef.

At this writing Michael is working as a saucier, responsible for preparing sauces and soups and assisting at the sauté station.

Alligators were once an endangered species, but now thrive in the web-like network of bayous, rivers, swamps and lakes along the Louisiana coast. They're sometimes found in park lagoons, drainage canals and other places near populated areas. Hunting or killing them requires a state license.

Antoine's was one of the first New Orleans restaurants to add alligator soup to their menus. Part of the motivation may have been that descendants of the restaurant's founder own acres of land bordering swamps and bayous.

As part of a group of Antoine's folk on an alligator hunt some time ago, I was too cautious to try my hand at bagging one on my own. But that hasn't discouraged me from enjoying a meal with the meat from an alligator that somebody else has caught.

(Recipe continued)
the stock and the browned alligator meat. Add a tablespoon of Creole seasoning and bring to a boil, stirring frequently. Reduce to low heat, cover with a lid and simmer for 45 minutes or until the meat is tender. Add salt to taste. Serve in soup or gumbo bowls and garnish with chopped green onion or parsley. At the table, pass dry sherry for each guest to drizzle into the soup.

ALLIGATOR SOUP WITH SHERRY

Alive, they're big, they're ugly and mean as all get out, but if you can secure one, alligator meat is a versatile component for sausage or soup. Many seafood suppliers on the internet offer prepared alligator sausage or dressed alligator meat.

The tail meat and the loin are also used in gumbos, sausage, and other regional seafood recipes. Alligator is a "mute" protein, which means it has little flavor of its own and relies on other ingredients for taste. The flavor is akin to that of chicken, with a slightly fishy undertone.

SERVES: 8 to 12

1 pound	boneless alligator tail meat		2	cloves garlic, minced
1/4 cup plus 1 tablespoon	Creole seasoning*		4 quarts	seafood or chicken stock**
1 1/2 cups, divided	unsalted butter		1	whole bay leaf
2 cups	white onion, chopped medium dice		1/2 teaspoon	dried thyme
1 cup	celery, chopped medium dice		1/2 teaspoon	dried oregano
1/3 cup	green bell pepper, chopped		1/2 teaspoon	dried basil
1 cup	all-purpose flour		1/4 cup	flat-leaf (Italian) parsley or green onions, chopped for garnish
3	fresh tomatoes peeled and crushed, or one 12-ounce can of Roma tomatoes		1/2 cup	dry sherry

* See page 93 for a Creole seasoning recipe.
** See page 85 for a chicken or seafood stock recipe.

DIRECTIONS

*Before preparing this recipe, read the instructions for making roux on pages 86-87.

Trim fat from alligator tail meat and cut the meat into 3-inch pieces. Using a kitchen mallet, pound the meat to tenderize it until it is about 1 inch thick. Cut these into smaller pieces about 1 inch square. Dust the meat lightly with Creole seasoning, about 1 grain deep.

Using a Dutch oven or other heavy bottomed pot, melt 3/4 cup of the butter over medium heat and brown the meat for 10 to 15 minutes. Stir occasionally to prevent sticking. Remove the browned meat and any browned drippings and set aside. Add the remaining 3/4 cup butter, the celery, green pepper and onion. Sauté until the onions are translucent and soft, about 5 minutes.

Make a roux by gradually sprinkling in flour and stirring to blend with the vegetables. Continue stirring and cook to light brown caramel color. Add tomatoes and garlic, and cook for 5 more minutes. Slowly add 3 cups of the stock and stir until roux and stock is combined. Add the rest of *(Continued on left)*

THE PREUSS FAMILY, BROUSSARD'S

Bouillabaisse

Bouillabaisse, a glorious blending of finfish and shellfish in a luscious broth, is the gift of the fishermen plying the waters of the Mediterranean near Marseilles. New Orleans restaurant chefs have long used the French original as the inspiration of a Creole version of the dish.

SERVES: 6 to 8

BROTH

1 cup each of	carrots , peeled, small-dice	1/2 cup	tomato paste
	celery ribs, small-dice	1 gallon	shrimp or fish stock*
	fennel, small-dice	2 cups	tomatoes chopped,
	yellow onions, small-dice		crushed and drained
	green bell pepper, small-dice	1/8 teaspoon	saffron threads
1 tablespoon	garlic, minced		kosher or sea salt, to taste
1/4 cup	French shallots, small-dice		white pepper, to taste
1/2 cup	olive oil	3	whole bay leaves

For a shrimp or fish sock recipe see page 85.

DIRECTIONS

In an 8-quart stockpot, heat the olive oil over high heat, and sauté the carrots, celery and fennel until they are cooked half-way.

In a small saucepan with a lid, bring 1/2 cup of water to a quick boil, then turn off heat. Add the saffron threads to the water to steep for approximately 15 minutes. Set saffron and water aside.

Add the onion, bell pepper, garlic and shallots to the pot. Heat the vegetables until the garlic and onions are semi-translucent. Add the tomato paste and cook over medium-high heat for 10 minutes, stirring often. While the vegetables are cooking, heat the shrimp or fish stock in a separate pot to lukewarm. Add the lukewarm stock, tomatoes, steeped saffron and saffron water, bay leaves and salt and pepper to taste. Bring to a full boil over high heat. Once boil is reached, remove from heat, cool, cover and chill in the refrigerator.

BOUILLABAISSE SEAFOOD

1 pound	raw shrimp (36 to 40 per pound), shelled and deveined	1/2 pound	skinless trout fillets, cut into 1-inch cubes
1 cup	raw oysters	1/2 pound	raw scallops
1/2 pound	jumbo lump crab meat, Louisiana blue crabs preferred	18	raw mussels in the shell, scrubbed
1/2 pound	crawfish tail meat		

Bring the prepared broth to a boil in an 8-quart stockpot. Add the shrimp, oysters, crab meat, crawfish, fish, scallops and mussels, and bring back to a simmer. Cook for 5 minutes, or until the seafood is cooked but is not tough.

Chef Gunter Preuss has every right to be proud of his special bouillabaisse, made from a treasured recipe. Broussard's restaurant, owned and operated by Gunter, his wife Evelyn, and their son Marc, is a French Quarter landmark, founded by the legendary Broussard brothers in 1920. The restaurant's classically elegant dining rooms partially enclose a large, lush courtyard that's a spectacular setting for cocktails on balmy evenings.

ROUILLE SPREAD

1 cup	bread crumbs
2 tablespoons	chimayo chile, chopped
1	whole garlic clove
3/4 cup	olive oil
1/2 tablespoon	lemon juice
24	crostini toasts

For the crostini, cut crusty French or Italian bread into small slices. Butter and toast the bread. For the rouille spread, place all ingredients except crostini toasts in a food processor or blender and pulse until smooth.

Divide the bouillabaisse broth equally among 6 to 8 shallow, gumbo-type bowls. Apportion the seafood attractively in the center of each bowl and serve with crostini and rouille on the side.

Generations of New Orleanians have been lured to Grand Isle, a thin strip of land southwest of the city where fishing camps rise mere yards from the Gulf of Mexico.

Many of the city dwellers went there to fish. For others, it was simply to gather around tables piled high with boiled crabs or shrimp while breathing some of the salty sea air. There's another Grand Isle, this one a creation of chef Joel Dondis in the New Orleans Warehouse District. The restaurant is one of Dondis' entrepreneurial successes, along with his other restaurant La Petite Grocery, the confectionery Sucré and Joel's Fine Catering.

CHILLED CREOLE TOMATO SOUP

If you're looking for a family name that's authentically south Louisiana, Falgoust should fill the bill. So it's only natural that the food turned out by Executive Chef Mark Falgoust at Grand Isle, in New Orleans' Warehouse District usually carries a south-Louisiana birth certificate. And what ingredient could better connect with the region's cuisine than the Creole tomatoes that identify this luscious soup?

SERVES: 6

8	small, ripe Creole* tomatoes
11 ounces	tomato juice
	juice from one fresh lime
1	Vidalia sweet onion, thinly sliced
1	jalapeño pepper, small dice
1	cucumber, small dice
1/2	yellow bell pepper, small dice

5	fresh basil leaves, minced
	kosher or sea salt, to taste
	black pepper, freshly ground to taste
6 ounces	cooked crawfish tails, optional
6 ounces	cooked shrimp, peeled, optional

*If Creole tomatoes are not available, use the ripest good-quality tomatoes you can find.

DIRECTIONS

With a sharp knife, cut an "X" in the bottom center of tomatoes and core them. Submerge them in boiling water for approximately 1 minute. Remove and rinse under cold water.

Peel the skin from the tomatoes, cut them in half horizontally and gently squeeze them to remove the seeds.

Place the tomatoes, tomato juice and lime juice in a food processor or blender and purée the mixture until well blended. Pour into a non-reactive container, one made of stainless steel, glass or ceramic. (Aluminum and copper will react chemically with the acids, affecting the color and taste of the tomatoes.)

Add all of the remaining ingredients, including seafood if used.

Refrigerate two hours to allow flavors to blend, or until chilled to the desired temperature.

CREAM OF GARLIC SOUP

Garlic and onions, caramelized and puréed, are the components that give this bread-thickened soup a lot of character. Chef Susan Spicer emphasizes that taking the time to cook the garlic and onions properly is essential. The mixture should be stirred regularly on low heat until it becomes very dark and caramelizes. A garnish of small croutons adds a delightful crunchy contrast to the soup's silkiness.

SERVES: 8

2 tablespoons	unsalted butter		1	bouquet garni** made with parsley stems, thyme sprigs, and bay leaf
2 tablespoons	olive oil			
2 pounds	onions, peeled and sliced		3 cups	stale French bread, torn into 1/2 inch pieces
2 cups	garlic cloves, peeled, but not chopped			
1 tablespoon	fresh thyme, chopped or 1 teaspoon dried		1 cup	half-and-half or heavy cream kosher or sea salt and black peppercorns freshly ground
7 cups	chicken stock* preferably home-made, divided			

*See page 85 for chicken-stock recipe.
** See page 92 for bouquet garni directions.

DIRECTIONS

Heat the butter and oil in a heavy-bottomed 2-quart saucepan or Dutch oven over medium-low heat. Add the onions and garlic and cook, stirring frequently, until they turn a deep golden brown, 30 to 40 minutes.

Add the thyme, 6 cups of the chicken stock, and the bouquet garni and bring to a boil. Stir in the bread cubes and let simmer for 10 minutes, until the bread is soft. Remove the soup from heat and cool for 10 minutes.

Remove the bouquet and purée the soup in a blender (in batches if necessary), until completely smooth. Return the soup to the pot and heat to the desired temperature.

Whisk in more chicken stock if the mixture is too thick. Add half-and-half or cream until the soup reaches the texture of a classic cream soup. Season to taste with salt and pepper.

As chefs go, Susan Spicer is an amazing example of creativity, tenacity and generosity.

She began preparing her acclaimed garlic soup as a fledgling cook at Louis XVI, perhaps to ward off French Quarter creatures of the night, or simply because it is an extraordinary recipe.

Susan has mentored many chefs, and placed her stamp of originality everywhere she has worked. She then opened Bayona, her own restaurant in the French Quarter. She has been honored by the James Beard Foundation as Best Chef Southeast 1993 and was named one of Food & Wine's *10 Best New Chefs.*

She partnered with Donald Link, her former executive sous chef, to create Herbsaint. There, as executive chef, he has also been honored by the James Beard Foundation as Best Chef Southeast 2007, but he doesn't serve garlic soup, although author Anne Rice made uptown vampires quite the norm.

There's a period during the summer when fresh Creole tomatoes and fresh corn are available at the same time. This is when New Orleanian Grace Bauer, an accomplished cook, writer and designer, heads for Becnel's produce stand in Plaquemines Parish, across the Mississippi River from the city.

With the tomatoes and corn she buys there, Grace makes a soup completely vegetarian-style by using vegetable stock rather than chicken stock in it.

The late Johnny Becnel was not only the New Orleans area's master Creole-tomato grower, he was also a rosarian, propagating many new roses, among them Cajun Sunrise and Cajun Moon, both of which are growing outside my kitchen.

GRACE BAUER

CREOLE TOMATO AND CORN SOUP

This versatile soup is produced "off season" by utilizing either fresh or canned corn and tomatoes, although fresh corn and Creole tomatoes are far superior. Flavors can be intensified with the judicious addition of other fresh herbs such as basil, dill or thyme.

SERVES: 6

4	ears fresh corn, or 2 (11-ounce) cans corn kernels	1/4 cup	celery, chopped
		1/8 teaspoon	cayenne pepper
		1 tablespoon	fresh thyme leaves, chopped
6	fresh, ripe Creole tomatoes, or 1 (14-1/2-ounce) can diced tomatoes, rinsed	1 1/2 quarts	chicken or vegetable stock
		6 tablespoons	unsalted butter
		5 tablespoons	all-purpose flour
1 tablespoon	vegetable oil	1 cup	heavy (or half & half) cream
3 tablespoons	garlic, minced	3 tablespoons	flat-leaf (Italian) parsley, minced for garnish
1/2 cup	medium yellow onion, diced		

DIRECTIONS

If using fresh ears of corn, bring a 2-quart saucepan of water to a boil, add the corn, return to a boil and cook for 10 minutes. Drain and cool. Using a sharp knife, scrape the kernels from the cob into a bowl and set aside.

If using fresh tomatoes, remove the skins by bringing a 2-quart saucepan, 2/3 filled with water, to a boil. Add the whole tomatoes and submerge for 30 to 45 seconds. Remove the tomatoes with a slotted spoon and run them under cold water. The skin will slip right off. Cut the cores from the tomatoes and set them aside.

Place the vegetable oil in a 2-quart saucepan over medium heat and slowly sauté the garlic until golden and aromatic. Stir in the onion and celery and continue to stir while cooking until the onion is transparent. Add the cayenne pepper and thyme leaves, then add the chicken stock and bring to a boil. Add half of the corn kernels to the stock and boil for 5 minutes. Purée the mixture, strain it, and allow it to cool.

In a large, heavy Dutch oven or very deep cast-iron skillet, make a blond roux* with the butter and flour, stirring and cooking over low heat for 8 to 10 minutes. Add the puréed corn and bring to a simmer. Add the cream and the remaining corn kernels and tomatoes, and cook for 5 minutes over medium heat. If the soup seems too thick, thin by adding more stock.

Ladle into serving bowls and garnish with parsley.

For information on making roux, see pages 86-87.

THE FOX FAMILY

Duck and Wild Rice Soup

When we smoke turkeys for Thanksgiving, we smoke ducks at the same time and set them aside for the following day. While roasted ducks probably would do just as well, that nice smoky flavor would be missing. In any event, use whichever cooking method you prefer for the ducks.

SERVES: 10 to 12

2	Muscovy ducks, each about 2 1/2 pounds, smoked or roasted	4	fresh garlic cloves, chopped
1 gallon	water	1/2 cup	parsley, chopped
1 gallon	chicken stock	1	carrot, roughly chopped
2	large white onions, roughly chopped	2	fresh rosemary sprigs
		6 ounces	wild rice
1	green bell pepper, roughly chopped	1 or 2	French baguette loaves
		1/2 cup	unsalted butter
3	celery stalks, roughly chopped	1 teaspoon	garlic powder
		1/4 cup	Parmigano-Reggiano cheese, grated
		1/8 cup	fresh rosemary, finely minced

DIRECTIONS

Remove the skin and pick the meat from the two ducks. Discard the skin and cut the duck meat into bite-size pieces. Set aside.

Split the duck carcasses in half. Set a 3-gallon stockpot over medium heat and pour in the water and chicken stock, then the onion, green bell pepper, celery, garlic, parsley, carrot and rosemary. Bring the liquid to a boil, then reduce the heat to medium and allow it to simmer one to two hours, until reduced by half. Periodically skim off the foam and impurities that float to the top.

Strain the stock and discard the carcasses and vegetables. Return the stock to the stockpot. Add the rice and simmer until it is fully cooked, approximately 1 hour. Add the duck meat and continue simmering until the gumbo is heated, about 15 minutes.

Preheat the oven to 350°F.

Cream together the butter, garlic powder, grated cheese and rosemary until the consistency is soft and smooth.

Slice the baguettes in half lengthwise and liberally butter the inside of each half. Place aluminum foil on a sheet tray and place bread in the center. Wrap loosely with aluminum foil. Warm in the oven about 15 minutes, until hot and crisp.

Serve in soup or gumbo bowls with the rosemary-garlic bread.

NEW ORLEANS

First sighted as Indian portage to Lake Pontchartrain and Gulf in 1699 by Bienville and Iberville. Founded by Bienville in 1718; named by him in honor of the Duke of Orleans, Regent of France. Called the Crescent City because of location in bend of the Mississippi.

Our brother-in-law, Glenn, would be most disappointed if duck soup were not on our four-day long Thanksgiving Festival menu. Patty, his wife and my sister, was born here, so it is a homecoming.

The family is evenly divided in preference for Robert's turkey andouille gumbo (see page 41) or Glenn's duck soup. They believe that the Thanksgiving Day turkeys and ducks are served simply to make gumbo and soup that evening.

Cleaning the kitchen is a continuous event, one we have nicely solved. There is a job jar on the counter. Anyone who enters must pull a task slip. It keeps the traffic down, but it also keeps the area tidied up.

On the occasion of Sue Zemanick's award as one of Food & Wine's Best New Chefs in America for 2008, the magazine commented that she "has imbued a 25-year-old New Orleans restaurant (Gautreau's) with fresh energy, deftly adding modern European touches to a classic menu."

A native of Wilkes-Barre, Penn., Sue graduated from the Culinary Institute of America and then joined the kitchen at the renowned Oceana restaurant in New York City.

Eventually, she found her way to New Orleans and a stint in the kitchen at Commander's Palace, before snagging the chef's position at Gautreau's, where she instantly gained a dedicated following among those diners who have a high regard for food that dovetails with New Orleans' own flavor profile yet brings to the table vibrant new approaches.

* See page 93 for a Creole seasoning recipe.

* See page 93 for a Creole seasoning recipe.

SUE ZEMANICK, GAUTREAU'S

OYSTER, LEEK AND POTATO SOUP WITH FRIED OYSTERS AND BACON

Fried oysters have become a favorite addition to any number of green salads in New Orleans, providing a wonderful counterpoint of flavor and texture. In this recipe, they garnish a rich but delicately flavored soup of leek and potato invigorated with white wine, oyster liquor, and aromatic herbs and seasonings.

SERVES: 10

SOUP

1/2 lb.	sliced applewood-smoked bacon			kosher or sea salt, to taste
2 tablespoons	unsalted butter			black pepper, freshly ground,
2 tablespoons	rendered fat from bacon			to taste
2	medium Idaho potatoes, diced		1 tablespoon	fresh thyme, chopped
1 cup	white onion, diced		1	whole bay leaf
1 1/2 cups	leek, white part only, diced		1 cup	dry white wine
1 cup	celery, diced		4 cups	vegetable stock
1/2 cup	French shallots, diced		2 cups	oyster liquid
2 cloves	garlic, roughly chopped			

DIRECTIONS

Fry the bacon slices until crisp. Crumble the bacon and set the bits aside for later use as garnish. Reserve the rendered bacon fat. Heat the butter and rendered bacon fat in a stock or soup pot over medium heat. Add the chopped potato, onion, leek, celery, shallots and garlic. Cook the vegetables until soft, stirring often, about 10 minutes.

Add the salt, pepper, thyme, bay leaf and wine. Cook the vegetables and seasonings until all wine has evaporated. Add the vegetable stock and oyster liquor and simmer the mixture for 15 minutes. Transfer the soup to a blender and purée it. Then strain it through a fine-mesh strainer.

FRIED OYSTERS

40	raw oysters, shucked		1/4 teaspoon	kosher or sea salt
1 cup	all-purpose flour		1/4 teaspoon	black pepper, freshly ground
1/2 cup	yellow cornmeal		4	egg whites
1 tablespoon	Creole seasoning*		1/2 gallon	peanut or canola oil

DIRECTIONS

Heat the oil to 350°F. Combine the flour, corn meal, Creole seasoning, salt and pepper in a bowl. Set aside. In a separate bowl, whip the egg whites until foamy and add the oysters. Strain off any excess egg white from each oyster and dredge each in the flour. Fry until crisp, about 1 to 2 minutes. To serve, garnish each bowl of soup with four oysters and bits of crumbled bacon.

LUMP CRAB MEAT AND BRIE SOUP

Fresh Louisiana crab meat partnered with Brie create a rich, creamy soup that performs well in a demitasse cup as a first course, or in a full bowl as a main dish.

YIELDS: 3 quarts

1 1/2 pounds	fresh, raw Louisiana hard-shell blue crabs	1 cup	white wine
2 ounces	melted butter	2 quarts	water
1	medium yellow onion chopped	1 quart	heavy whipping cream
		1/2 cup	unsalted butter
1	medium carrot, chopped	3/4 cup	all-purpose flour
3	celery stalks, chopped	8 ounces	Brie cheese
1	garlic pod, minced	1 pinch	white pepper, freshly ground
2	whole bay leaves		
1/4 cup	brandy	1 pinch	cayenne pepper
		1 pinch	salt
		1/2 pound	jumbo lump crab meat, picked over for shells

DIRECTIONS

Crack open the crabs' shells with a heavy mallet or hammer. Heat the butter in a saucepan and sauté the crabs for 5 minutes. Add the onion, carrot, celery, garlic and bay leaves. Continue to sauté for 3 to 4 minutes.

Add the brandy, white wine and water and bring the stock to a simmer over medium heat. Cook for 30 minutes. Remove the crabs and vegetables from the pan and add the heavy cream to the stock.

In a separate, small sauté skillet melt the butter and blend in the flour until the mixture is smooth and creamy. Simmer over low heat for 1 minute. Once the stock with cream has come to a low simmer add the flour and butter mixture to the stock while constantly stirring. Cook for 4 to 5 minutes.

Remove and discard the outside rind from the Brie. Cut the cheese into 1-inch cubes and add them to the stock, stirring constantly, until the cheese completely dissolves.

Season the soup to taste with salt, white pepper and cayenne pepper. Strain the soup through a fine strainer, add the jumbo lump crab meat and serve.

Add "North" to "Dakota" and you have the name of chef Kim Kringlie's former home state. But by the time he and business partner Kenny LaCour opened Dakota's doors in late 1990, Kim had been thoroughly "Creolized," producing some of the most spirited and appealing south Louisiana dishes in the region.

For almost two decades the restaurant has pointed the way toward exceptional dining across Lake Pontchartrain from New Orleans. And, somehow, Kim has never run out of new ideas. He's one of the many exceptional chefs who've come to Louisiana to enrich its restaurant culture with daring and imagination.

Chef Greg Reggio began his cooking career as an apprentice at LeRuth's. He recalls with fondness his days on the restaurant's kitchen line, and credits his time there alongside pioneering chef Warren LeRuth with providing the inspiration and training he needed to succeed in his own right.

Greg is now a member of the Taste Buds, a trio of chefs who have developed innovative recipes at such ground-breaking restaurants as their Semolina, Zea Rotisserie & Grill and Semolina's Bistro Italia. Chefs Gary Darling and Hans Limburg are his partners.

(Recipe continued)

Add the heavy cream, bring to a boil and simmer for 5 minutes. Whisk in enough of the roux to bring the thickness to that of cake batter. Add in all of the reserved oyster liquid and enough shrimp stock to thin the soup to a medium thick consistency, using up to 1 cup of shrimp stock to your preference. Cook for 5 minutes at a simmer. Adjust salt if necessary.

Just before serving, add the oysters, artichoke hearts and green onions.

This soup freezes well.

Oyster and Artichoke Soup

When, in the 1960s, the late and legendary Warren LeRuth introduced oyster and artichoke soup to the world at his namesake restaurant across the Mississippi River from New Orleans, the dish became an instant classic. "The inspiration for this recipe," says Greg Reggio, "comes from my mother's oyster stew that highlighted the simple fresh oyster flavors and buttery finish, and from my first professional cooking job at LeRuth's." We think Warren would be proud of Greg's takeoff on his creation.

SERVES: 10 to 12

1 1/2 sticks	unsalted butter, divided		1 teaspoon	fresh thyme
	all-purpose flour, as needed		2 cups	heavy cream
1 quart	shucked raw oysters, with juices			shrimp stock,* as needed
1 cup	yellow onion, diced (1/4-inch)			up to 1 cup
1/2 cup	celery, diced (1/4-inch)			kosher, or sea salt, to taste
2 teaspoons	garlic, minced		1/2 cup	green onion, sliced (1/4-inch)
2 tablespoons	parsley, finely chopped		2 cups	artichoke hearts, chopped**
1 tablespoon	Paul Prudhomme's Blackened Redfish Magic, or another low-salt Cajun spice blend			

See page 85 for shrimp-stock recipe.
**If you cannot find fresh baby artichoke hearts, substitute frozen hearts, which are much better than most canned artichokes.*

DIRECTIONS

Before preparing this recipe, read the instructions for making roux on pages 86-87.

Begin by making a blond roux. Melt 1 stick of butter in a heavy, 6-to-8-quart pot over medium heat. Whisk in enough flour to bring the texture of the mixture to that of wet sand. Cook the roux until the color becomes a light tan and the aroma is somewhat nutty. Do not brown the roux. Remove the roux from the pot and set aside.

Place the oysters and their juices in a saucepan. Cook just until the oysters are plump and their edges fan out. Be careful to not overcook them. Remove the poached oysters from the liquid and spread them out on a sheet pan to cool. Reserve the liquid. Once the oysters are cool enough to handle, cut them into 1/2-to-3/4-inch pieces.

In another pan, blanch the artichoke hearts in boiling water until tender. Allow them to cool and cut them into 1/2-inch pieces.

Melt the remaining butter in the skillet. Add the onion, celery, garlic and parsley. Cook over medium heat until the onion is translucent and the celery is tender. Do not brown the vegetables.

(Continued on left)

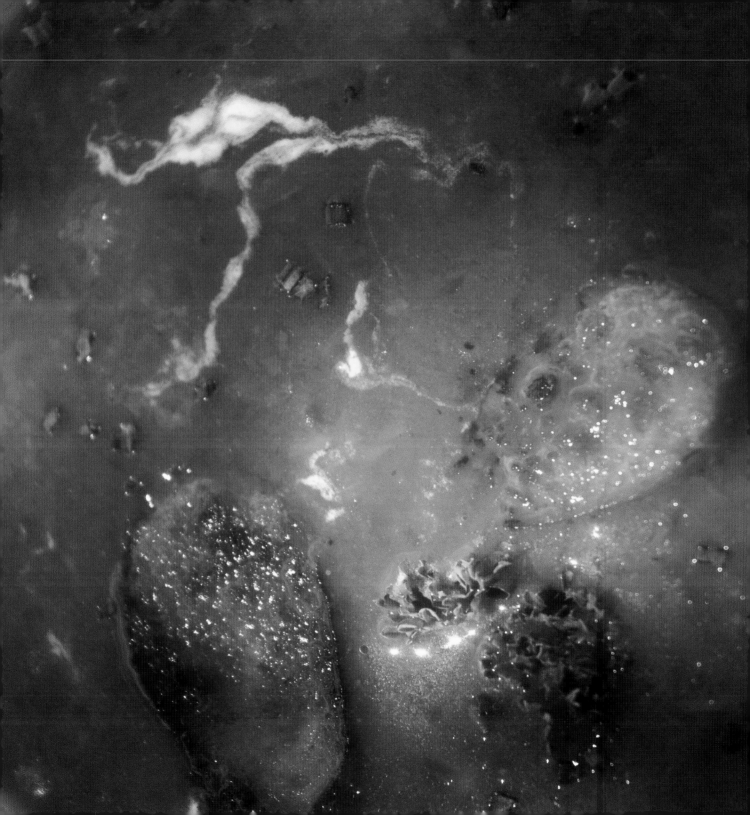

BILLY WOHL

RED BEAN AND SAUSAGE SOUP

As far back as anybody can remember, red beans and rice have been a traditional Monday meal in New Orleans. The dish also can make a comeback later in the week as an ingredient in chili, an omelet, a canapé spread or a red bean soup like this hearty one.

In lieu of red beans prepared from scratch, we often use the Blue Runner brand of canned red beans. Also, we occasionally ship cases of Blue Runner beans to expatriate New Orleanians who long for a taste of home.

SERVES: 6 to 8

2	16-ounce cans Blue Runner red beans, or 4 cups of prepared red beans	1/2 cup	cheddar cheese, grated
1 tablespoon	unsalted butter	1 pound	smoked or kielbasa sausage
1	yellow onion, finely chopped		kosher or sea salt, to taste
1	sprig fresh thyme		black pepper, freshly ground to taste
1	whole bay leaf		sour cream, for garnish
2 quarts	chicken stock, home-made if possible*, unsalted		chopped parsley, for garnish or green onion, for garnish

*See page 85 for a chicken stock recipe.

DIRECTIONS

Warm the red beans in a 4-to-6 quart saucepan or Dutch oven. In a seperate small saucepan, melt the butter over medium heat. Add the onion, and thyme, and sauté until the onion is softened, about 5 to 7 minutes. Stir the mixture into the beans and add the bay leaf. Add the stock and cheddar cheese. After simmering the soup for about 1/2 hour, remove the bay leaf and set aside.

Cut the sausage into 1/4-inch slices. Fry it with a little water in a skillet until browned. Remove the sausage and set aside.

In batches, purée the soup in a blender and then mash it through a sieve into a clean saucepan. Return the soup to medium-high heat and add salt and pepper, stirring and tasting as you go until the seasonings are right.

Add the sausage slices to the soup and reduce the heat to a slow simmer until ready to serve.

Ladle the soup into wide, shallow serving bowls. Garnish each serving with a dollop of sour cream and a sprinkle of chopped parsley or green onion. Serve immediately.

Billy, my husband, embraces the notion that cooking is to splash a bit of wine, beer or brandy into a pot already simmering on the stove. His red bean soup is an exception. If his beans are served with rice, he prefers them soupy, which is no doubt why he came up with this recipe.

The addition of cheddar cheese to the simmering stock adds body as a flavor enhancer. The cheese itself doesn't deliver a taste of its own but it intensifies the flavors of the other ingredients.

Occasionally, Billy will grate cheese and finely chopped onion as a garnish, similar to what's done with black bean soup. Add a loaf of crisp, hot French bread and a salad and this is a meal.

Chef Austin Leslie inspired "Frank's Place", an offbeat CBS sitcom in 1987-88 based on his restaurant, Chez Hélène. His sideburns and captain's hat added flavor to the show.

African-American neighborhoods celebrated restaurants such as Chez Hélène, Dooky Chase's, and Eddie's. Chef Leslie elevated Creole cooking through French and African influences, creating a number of signature recipes.

Chef Leslie closed Chez Hélène, and joined Jacques-Imo's, a funky uptown establishment well suited to his flair. He moved on to Pampy's, where he held the highest office in the kitchen.

Hurricane Katrina closed Pampy's and Chef Leslie evacuated to Atlanta, where he retired but was ready to get back to work, until his last meal was served in 2005.

His was the first New Orleans jazz funeral following Katrina. It honored him, winding past restaurants and marching him toward a different heavenly repast. Here on earth you can still get Chef Leslie's sweet potato soup, if you make it yourself.

AUSTIN LESLIE

Sweet Potato Soup

Surprisingly, sweet potato soup is not very sweet. The sweetness of the potatoes is tempered by the addition of onion and bacon.

YIELDS: 1 1/2 quarts or 8 servings

3 large	sweet potatoes		1/2 teaspoon	kosher or sea salt
3 tablespoons	unsalted butter		1/2 teaspoon	white pepper, freshly ground
1 tablespoon	granulated sugar		1 teaspoon	nutmeg, grated
1/3	onion, chopped			parsley, chopped, for garnish
2	bacon slices			nutmeg, grated, for garnish
3 cups	chicken stock*		1/2 cup	sherry, optional
1 cup	light cream			

*See page 85 for a chicken stock recipe.

DIRECTIONS

Preheat the oven to 350°F.

Pierce the sweet potatoes with a fork and place them in the oven on a foil-lined sheet pan for about 1 hour or until they are soft and a fork completely pierces one easily. Set them aside to cool.

When the sweet potatoes are cool enough to handle, peel them and cut them into 1-inch pieces. Place the cubes in a 2-quart bowl and mash them with butter and sugar.

Fry the bacon slices in a deep skillet and set them aside on a paper towel to drain. Sauté the onion in the rendered bacon drippings. Add 2 cups chicken stock, 1 cup cream and the salt, white pepper and nutmeg. Bring to a boil, lower heat and simmer for 5 minutes.

Add the sweet potatoes and purée all ingredients in a blender or food processor. Add the extra cup of chicken stock gradually until the desired consistency is reached. If the sweet potatoes are stringy, strain the soup through a colander and return it to the pot. Crumble the drained bacon. Return the soup to a medium heat and bring it to serving temperature.

Place the soup in serving bowls and drizzle each with the optional sherry. Sprinkle each bowl of soup lightly with nutmeg and garnish with crumbled bacon and chopped parsley.

© Photograph Rolfe Tessem

LINDA ELLERBEE
FRENCH BREAD AND TOMATO SOUP

South Louisiana's distinctively flavored Creole tomatoes usually first appear in early June, with the season ending four to six weeks later. This soup, which is a meal in itself, is a great excuse to celebrate the season—for brunch, lunch or a Sunday evening supper. If Creole tomatoes are out of season or out of reach, use canned tomatoes.

SERVES: 4 to 6

2	tablespoons extra-virgin olive oil, for sautéing		black peppercorns, freshly ground to taste
1	medium white onion, chopped	4	large eggs
4	garlic cloves, minced	1/2	loaf stale French bread roughly torn into 12 chunks
3	large Creole tomatoes, peeled, or a 28-ounce can of good-quality tomatoes	1/2 cup	to 1 cup Parmigiano-Reggiano cheese, grated
1 cup	dry white wine	3 tablespoons	fresh basil, chopped
2 quarts	chicken stock,** fresh if possible, unsalted	1/4 cup	extra-virgin olive oil, for garnish
	kosher or sea salt to taste	1/8 cup	balsamic vinegar, for garnish

See page 85 for a chicken stock recipe.
**Prepared chicken stock is sometimes salted. Consequently, look for the low-sodium kind and do not salt the soup until ready to eat.*

DIRECTIONS

In a 3- to 4-quart Dutch oven or a similarly sized heavy pot, sauté the onion and garlic in the olive oil until soft and translucent. If using fresh tomatoes, drop them into a separate pot of boiling water for 30 seconds to loosen skins, then remove and run them under cold water. The skins will slip off easily. Core the tomatoes, and using your hands, crush them. Add them to the garlic and onions. Cook for another 60 seconds. Add the white wine and simmer for another 30 seconds. Add chicken stock, bring to a boil then reduce heat to simmer for 20 minutes.

Poach 1 egg for each serving. To easily poach eggs, fill a large skillet or saucepan up to 1 or 2 inches, or enough water to cover the eggs. Bring water to a simmer over low heat. Break each egg into the simmering water, keeping it separate from the others. Using a large spoon, baste each egg gently with the water to cook the tops, if necessary. Remove the skillet from heat and set aside.

Place 3 chunks of French bread into the bottom of each bowl. Pour soup on top of the bread to cover completely. Using a slotted spoon, carefully remove a poached egg from the skillet and slip onto each bowl of soup.

To finish, top with a generous sprinkle of grated Parmigiano-Reggiano cheese and fresh chopped basil. Drizzle with a little extra virgin olive oil, and a splash balsamic vinegar. Add a grind of fresh pepper. Season to taste with salt, and then serve.

There are two important things to know about Linda Jane Ellerbee: She loves New Orleans and she loves to cook. She also loves to serve, eat and talk about food when she's not making television shows or books happen. The kitchen is Linda's notion of heaven, and hers is overseen by a framed photograph of herself together with her guardian angel, Julia Child.

When she visits New Orleans, nothing makes Linda happier than to visit the Crescent City Farmers' Market on Magazine Street early on a Saturday morning, then to assume control of somebody's kitchen, and finally feed hungry people.

When, on a certain Saturday, she discovered the baskets of Creole tomatoes at the market just waiting for her attention, she grabbed them and created this recipe by adapting an old recipe for a peasant soup, one probably made with what was available at a farm. This kind of kitchen improvising is certainly an important New Orleans tradition, and Linda has proven to be a master of the improviser's art.

TURTLE SOUP

In the kitchen at Commander's Palace, farm-raised, alligator-snapping turtles are used for this soup. A fresh-water species of turtle also is available all year along the Gulf Coast. Using wild turtle is illegal, but farm-raised is fine. Turtle meat is usually sold frozen in 2 1/2-pound portions, so this recipe is written to use that quantity. The meat freezes well (as does the soup) and can be ordered by mail or on the Internet.

SERVES: 6

1 1/2 sticks	butter	2 quarts	veal stock
2 1/2 pounds	turtle meat,* cut in a medium dice	1 cup	all-purpose flour
	kosher salt and freshly ground pepper to taste	1	750-milliliter bottle of dry sherry
2	medium onions, in medium dice	1 tablespoon	hot sauce, or to taste
6	celery stalks, in medium dice	1/4 cup	Worcestershire sauce
1	large head garlic, cloves peeled and minced	2	large lemons, juiced
3	bell peppers, any color, in medium dice	3 cups	fresh tomatoes, peeled, seeded and coarsely chopped
1 tablespoon	ground dried thyme	10 ounces	fresh spinach, washed thoroughly, stems removed and coarsely chopped
1 tablespoon	ground dried oregano	6	medium eggs, hard-boiled and chopped into large pieces
4	whole bay leaves		

*Beef or a combination of lean beef and veal stew meat may be substituted for the turtle meat
Before preparing this recipe, read the instructions for making roux on pages 86-87.

DIRECTIONS

Melt 4 tablespoons of the butter in a large soup pot over medium to high heat. Brown the meat in the hot butter. Season with salt and pepper, and cook for about 18 to 20 minutes, or until the liquid is almost evaporated. Add the onions, celery, garlic and peppers, stirring constantly. Then add the thyme, oregano and bay leaves and sauté for 20 to 25 minutes, until the vegetables have caramelized. Add the stock, bring to a boil, lower the heat and simmer uncovered for 30 minutes, periodically skimming away any fat that rises to the top.

While the stock is simmering, make a roux in a separate pot: Melt the remaining 8 tablespoons of butter over medium heat in a small saucepan and add the flour a little at a time, stirring constantly with a wooden spoon. Be careful not to burn the roux. After all the flour has been added, cook for about 3 minutes until the roux smells nutty, is pale in color, and has the consistency of wet sand. Set aside until the soup is ready.

Using a whisk, vigorously stir the roux into the soup a little at a time to prevent lumping. Simmer for about 25 minutes. Stir to prevent sticking on the bottom. Add the sherry and bring the liquid to a boil. Add the hot sauce and worcestershire and simmer, skimming any fat or foam that rises to the top. Add juice from the lemons and the tomatoes, and return to a simmer. Add the spinach and the chopped egg. Return to a simmer and adjust salt and pepper as needed.

Ella Brennan, matriarch of the Commander's Palace branch of the Brennan restaurant family, was an innovative restaurateur before her retirement. Among her many contributions to New Orleans' restaurant culture is the three-soup course. The trio is presented together in demitasse cups, providing a diner with a few sips of each. The idea has been copied in many of the city's other restaurants.

The trio of demitasses at Commander's normally includes the turtle soup, whatever gumbo is on the day's menu, and either the soup du jour or an oyster or shrimp bisque, although the combination follows no strict rule. Preparing three soups in one day may be daunting in some kitchens, but they can be made in advance, allowing their flavors to meld in the refrigerator for a day or two.

This recipe calls for the sherry to be incorporated into the turtle soup as it cooks. In other recipes the sherry is withheld until serving time, when a splash or two is added. Some guests prefer no sherry at all. It's simply a matter of taste.

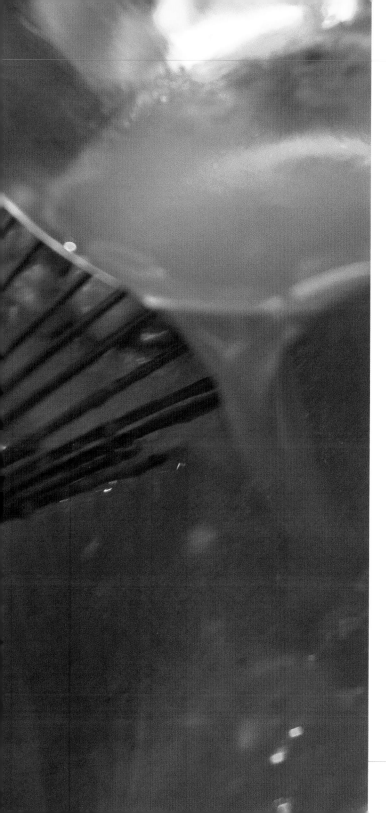

BASIC STOCKS

When a soup or stew is on the menu, it makes perfect sense that the liquid used to make it should bring as much to the flavor profile as the other ingredients and be as tasty as possible. And nothing puts razzmatazz in a soup or stew like a great, well balanced stock.

Chefs place a great deal of importance on stocks. Most hearty sauces begin with a stock reduction. When stocks are reduced, they become liquid gold—intense, deeply flavored potions that are revered by chefs and smart cooks. One of the key positions in a restaurant kitchen brigade is that of the saucier; that is, the sauce cook, to whom stocks are completely indispensable.

A stock is one of the easiest things that can be made on a stove. It may be used immediately or frozen in portions for future use. It troubles me when a soup recipe calls for adding a gallon of water, since, unlike stock, it adds no flavor or depth. While stocks take time to simmer, they do not require much effort. A stock is a strained liquid, and the happy result of cooking combinations of vegetables, meat or fish and other seasoning ingredients in water.

The most often used ingredients are simple—meaty bones, seafood shells, aromatic vegetables, and seasonings and spices. The bones provide the protein flavors. Celery, onion, bell pepper, carrot, herbs, salt and pepper contribute their own distinctive tastes.

Browning bones, vegetables and other ingredients before they're cooked in the liquid makes brown stock. Boiling a stock reduces the volume as the liquid evaporates, and creates a reduction. It intensifies the flavor and helps thicken the result. Reductions are grand to keep in small freezer containers, ready to heighten the flavor of a sauce or gravy.

Since stocks are strained to remove impurities, a lot of chopping is not necessary, and handfuls of celery tops and other odd vegetable trimmings are useful. Items that would normally wind up in the garbage or compost heap are valuable and budget-friendly.

Removing excess fat from meat stocks can be child's play. It's done by refrigerating the stock overnight in a covered container and allowing the fat to rise to the top and thicken. Removing it is simply a matter of skimming the fat off with a shallow-bowled spoon or a ladle.

Making a stock can be extremely simple with some advance planning. Many bones, shells and vegetable trimmings from the cutting board that are usually tossed into the garbage are excellent candidates for flavoring stocks. They can perform double duty by being tossed into the freezer instead, and then being quickly retrieved at stock-making time. Another time-saver is to make extra stock whenever you're preparing one for a recipe, and then freeze the surplus in 1-cup batches.

CHICKEN STOCK   YIELDS: 1 1/2 quarts

5 pounds	cooked chicken bones
1	large yellow onion, peeled and quartered
1	large carrot, c1ut into thirds
2	celery stalks, including leaves, cut into thirds
2	large or 4 small leeks, white and tender green parts cut in half lengthwise and well washed
2	whole bay leaves
6 sprigs	fresh flat-leaf (Italian) parsley
2 sprigs	fresh rosemary
1/2 teaspoon	dried thyme or a sprig of fresh thyme
12	whole black peppercorns

Place all ingredients in an 8-quart stockpot and cover with cold water. Bring to a boil over high heat. As the stock approaches a boil, begin carefully skimming impurities that form at the top with a ladle. Reduce heat and simmer, partially covered, for 3 to 4 hours, continuing to skim impurities form time to time while the stock cooks.

Taste after 3 hours for the strength of stock you want. Remove from the heat and let stand for 10 to 15 minutes, then ladle through a fine strainer. Cool by placing the container of strained stock in an ice water bath.

Once the stock is strained and cooled, skim the fat from it, then refrigerate it. If it is left in the refrigerator overnight, the fat will rise to the top and thicken, making it easily removable with a spoon or ladle. The stock will keep for about 1 week in the refrigerator. Any surplus can be frozen in 1-cup batches.

CRAB STOCK   YIELDS: 1 quart

5	whole raw Louisiana blue "gumbo crabs,"* cleaned and quartered for cooking
1	medium yellow onion, chopped
1/2 cup	chopped leeks, green tops only
1	clove garlic, finely chopped
1/2 cup	chopped celery
1	whole bay leaf
1 teaspoon	whole black peppercorns
6 cups	water
2 tablespoons	vegetable oil

Hard-shell crabs that are too small or scrawny to be picked for meat lumps.

In a 1-gallon stockpot over medium heat, sauté the onion, leek, garlic and celery in the oil for 3 to 5 minutes, until the onion is transparent. Add the crabs and all other ingredients and simmer for 1 to 1 1/2 hours, skimming the top to remove impurities throughout the cooking time. Strain the stock, allow it to cool.

SEAFOOD STOCK   YIELDS: 4 quarts

2 pounds	any combination of fish trimmings, shrimp, crab, lobster or crawfish shells, and whole raw Louisiana blue "gumbo crabs," cleaned and quartered
2	medium yellow onions, coarsely chopped
2	large or 4 small leeks, white and green parts cut in half lengthwise and well washed
2	celery stalks, including tops, coarsely chopped
4	whole bay leaves
1 teaspoon	dried thyme
1 1/2 teaspoons	whole white peppercorns
1	whole garlic head, cut in half horizontally
4 quarts	very cold water

Place all ingredients in a large stockpot. Bring to a boil. (Do not allow the stock to boil rapidly, or it will turn cloudy.) As the stock approaches a boil, begin carefully skimming impurities that form at the top with a ladle. Reduce heat and simmer, partially covered, for 45 minutes. After removing the stock from heat, strain it and allow it to cool before using.

SHRIMP STOCK   YIELDS: 2 quarts

2 to 3 cups	raw shrimp shells and heads
3 quarts	water

Place the shrimp heads and shells in a large pot and cover with the water. Bring to a boil over high heat, then lower the heat and simmer gently until the amount of liquid is reduced to 2 quarts. Strain through a fine-mesh strainer.

VEGETABLE STOCK   YIELDS: 2 quarts

2 tablespoons	vegetable oil
1 bunch	green onions, chopped
2	medium yellow onions, roughly chopped
3	celery stalks, cut into 2-inch pieces
9 cups	water
6	medium carrots, cut into 1-inch pieces
2	garlic cloves, peeled and crushed
6	fresh parsley sprigs, with
2	whole bay leaves

Clean, chop and cut the vegetables then set aside. Heat the oil in a stockpot or 5-quart Dutch oven over medium-high heat. Add the onions and celery and simmer for 5 minutes, or until vegetables are translucent. Add water, carrots, garlic, parsley, pepper and bay leaves. Bring the stock to a boil over high heat, then reduce the heat to medium-low. Simmer, uncovered, for 1 1/2 hours. Remove the stock from heat, cool slightly and strain it through a large sieve or colander over a large bowl. Press the vegetables lightly against sides of the sieve or colander to remove excess liquid. Discard the vegetables. The stock is ready for use.

Roux and the "Trinity"

Roux is the magical thickener and flavoring necessary for many gumbos, stews and soups in Louisiana cooking. Making roux is not nearly as difficult as it may sound and can approach a Zen-like experience for a dedicated cook. Depending on skill and speed, creating a light ("blond") roux can take a few minutes and a dark roux up to 45 minutes or an hour. The great news is that roux freezes beautifully. So make a large batch, cool it, then apportion it into small containers and freeze it for future use.

A roux is nothing more than flour browned in oil or fat, and it delivers much more flavor than that would suggest. The raw flour taste is eliminated in the final product, and the chemical reaction created by the flour browning in the hot oil imparts a nutty, smoky flavor that deepens as the roux becomes darker. The scent as the reaction begins is distinctive and appetizing.

A Creole or Cajun roux begins with flour and oil or fat in equal proportions. Some cooks prefer a thicker roux, using more flour than oil.

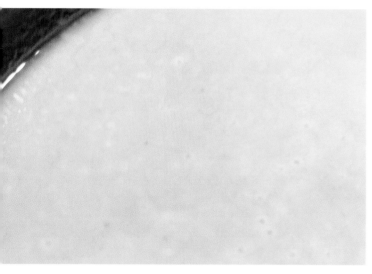

The language of roux pertains to its different hues, which can range from a barely colored tan to the color of peanut butter and through café au lait to dark mahogany. Before choosing the oil or fat, decide on the flavor and color of roux you're seeking. For example, a blond roux's flavor is more subtle but has higher thickening power than a dark roux.

The appropriate cooking medium is anything from vegetable oil, olive oil or canola oil to bacon grease, Crisco or lard. Butter burns easily at low temperatures, so unless it is clarified and the solids skimmed off, it will not work easily for a darker roux.

While white all-purpose flour is the norm, whole-wheat flour imparts a splendid nutty taste. The 1-to-1 ratio of oil and flour is standard, although some cooks prefer a bit more flour than oil, as much as 1/2 a cup on a one cup to one cup measurement.

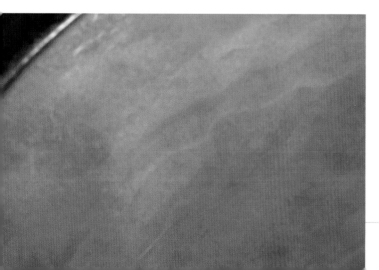

Begin the process by turning on some music (for entertainment while you're stirring) and assembling the necessary equipment. The ideal basic tools are a comfortable wire whisk and a cast-iron skillet or Dutch oven. Thin metal pots significantly increase the risk of scorching.

Start the roux by heating the oil on medium-low heat. Once the flour is added, stir the mixture continuously with a whisk. Be patient and take your time. Once the oil and flour begin to emulsify and bubble, the heat level can be raised or lowered. But this calls for diligence. The color stays deceptively the same for some minutes, then changes rapidly.

The flour can scorch before you're able to react. (There is no saving a scorched roux. It is over, it is finished, and it must be trashed.) So, once the roux starts to approach the desired color level, remove it from the flame a shade or two lighter than you want and continue whisking, since the flour will continue to cook quickly and darken further.

If the roux stands for an appreciable amount of time before it's used, and the oil separates and floats to the top, simply pour or skim off the oil. What happens when the oil floats to the top of the gumbo and does not emulsify? The roux, vegetables and stock are probably at different temperatures when they are finally combined, or an abundance of oil has been used, some from added ingredients.

If you're using such other fatty ingredients as sausage, precook and drain them before adding them to the gumbo. The oils that are released may be excellent flavoring for making the roux. In the final analysis, as the gumbo simmers, carefully skim off any excess oil or fat.

A simple method to control the consistency of the gumbo is to heat the stock and have it simmering in another pot. Then reverse the method. Instead of adding the stock to the roux, add the roux to the stock, using a wire whisk. Chefs tend to prefer this method of adding only the amount of roux required, allowing more control over the thickness.

THE "TRINITY"

If you intend to use the roux for gumbo, you'll want to add the "Trinity" of Creole-Cajun cooking—chopped onion, celery and bell pepper. While the addition of these vegetables will cause the roux to darken, it also begins cooling the roux as the vegetables cook and release their liquids. Once the vegetables have softened, gradually begin stirring in the stock or other liquid.

STOVE-TOP ROUX WITH THE TRINITY

The proportions among the Trinity's components can vary according to the cook's fancy, as well as the cook's personal preferences among them and what happens to be in the refrigerator at a given moment.

Essentially, however, the Trinity is:

2 parts	onion, chopped
1 part	celery, chopped
1/3 part	green* bell pepper, chopped

These days, many recipes call for bell peppers in their confetti colors of green, yellow, red and orange. There are no flavor or textural differences among them, so use whichever you prefer.

Once the vegetables are chopped, combined and set aside, prepare the roux.

When the roux has been cooked to a shade or two under what you're seeking, carefully begin stirring in the Trinity. When the vegetables hit the hot roux they will splatter, so add them slowly and stand back from the skillet. When the vegetables have been completely incorporated into the roux, the flour will darken even more. Allow the mixture to simmer until the vegetables release their liquids and the onions are translucent.

At this point, slowly add the stock or water, stirring as it is blended. Louisiana cookbook author Marcelle Bienvenu, whose vast experience makes her an expert in these matters, prefers to heat the liquid before adding it. This works well.

From the very beginning of the cooking process, the quality of the roux, Trinity and stock is most important for a gumbo's full-bodied flavor.

A word of caution about seafood gumbo: Reserve the delicately flavored raw oysters, shrimp, fish or crawfish until the gumbo is just a few minutes from being removed from heat. Otherwise, the seafood will overcook and become tough and tasteless. The same applies to other proteins such as sausage, chicken and duck. Give them enough time to cook at the end, but don't leech out their flavor by overcooking.

The stove-top method is the one I always use in making roux. Other cooks use a different method, either cooking it in a microwave oven or browning it in a stove oven. Both methods require some stirring during the process.

MICROWAVE ROUX

Yields: 2 cups

1 cup	all-purpose flour
1 cup	vegetable oil (preferred), lard or shortening
1/2 cup	water

In an uncovered, 1-quart glass container, mix the flour and oil together until smooth. Microwave on high. After 5 to 6 minutes and stir thoroughly. Continue microwaving for periods of 30 seconds until the desired color is reached. Stir at the end of each 30-second microwaving.

The traditional "trinity" of chopped green seasonings—onion, celery and sweet green pepper—may be added now, in an amount equal to those of the flour and oil.

Add 1 cup of water, mix everything thoroughly and continue microwaving, stirring occasionally, for an additional 5 minutes, or until the vegetables are soft and the onions are translucent.

Skim off any oil that remains on the surface.

OVEN-BAKED ROUX

The following recipe underscores my prejudice about oven-baked roux, in that it requires interrupting what you're doing every 15 minutes. A kitchen timer is recommended for this recipe.

Preheat oven to 400°F.

Yields: 2 cups

2 cups	all-purpose flour
2 cups	vegetable oil

In a large, heavy (preferably cast-iron) skillet, mix the flour and oil until smooth.

Place the skillet uncovered in the center of the oven for 1 to 2 hours, depending on the darkness of the color you wish to achieve. Stir every 15 minutes until the desired color has been reached.

Skim off any oil that remains on the surface.

RICE

Rice can be almost as important an ingredient in gumbo as roux. A lot of personal opinions have floated around about the best method for cooking rice. The only right one is yours. That being said, there are major fans of the rice cooker, which, I am told, delivers perfectly cooked rice every time. I am divesting myself of gadgets and odd appliances, so if you are fortunate enough to own a rice cooker, enjoy.

The cooking method I once used for rice is quite simple. Use two cups of water or chicken stock to one cup of rice, either long or short grain. (In Louisiana we tend to prefer the long grain.)

MOIST RICE

SERVES: 6 to 8 for gumbo

2 cups	water or chicken stock
1/2 teaspoon	kosher or sea salt
1 tablespoon	unsalted butter
1 cup	raw white rice, long or short grain

DIRECTIONS

In a 1-quart saucepan add the salt, butter and rice. When the water begins to a boil, cover the pot with a tight-fitting lid, lower the temperature to a simmer and allow it to cook for 15 to 20 minutes.

If the water or rice measurements are off, the moon is full or it is an alternate Sunday, it can clump into sticky rice.* Check it by biting into a few grains. If they are cooked through, the rice is done. Overcooking can result in very dry rice that can scorch. (To prevent scorching I move the covered rice pot to a cold burner for the last 5 minutes to allow it to steam and finish on its own.)

At our house, this method can be controversial. I adore sticky rice. My husband prefers his in separate, beautifully cooked grains. A friend finally taught me her secret for making the rice my husband prefers.

DRY RICE

SERVES: 6 to 8 for gumbo

1 cup	white rice, long or short grain
1 quart	water or chicken stock
1 tablespoon	butter
1/2 teaspoon	kosher or sea salt

DIRECTIONS

Place the quart of water in a 2-quart saucepan and bring to the boiling point. Add the rice, salt and butter. Bring back to a boil and cover with a tightly fitting lid. Allow the rice to boil for 10 to 15 minutes, or until it is completely cooked when you bite into a grain.

Drain the rice in a colander and rinse with cold water. Rinse out the 2-quart saucepan and fill it again half-way with water. Bring the water to a boil and place the colander on top to steam until the rice is warm.

Cooked rice can be put into sealable plastic bags and refrigerated for use within two days or frozen for future use. Simply steam until warm.

OVEN BAKED RICE

SERVES: 6 to 8 for gumbo

2 ounces	clarified butter or olive oil
1 cup	rice, preferably long grain
2 cups	water or stock of choice
	kosher or sea salt to taste
	freshly ground black pepper to taste
	bouquet garni (see page 92)

DIRECTIONS

Preheat oven to 450°F

Using a Dutch oven over medium heat on the stovetop, stir rice and oil for about 3 minutes.

Place in preheated oven without disturbing for 20 minutes.

The rice will absorb the liquid. If it is still moist, continue to cook for an additional five minutes in the oven or remove from oven and cover with a lid and allow to stand. Discard the bouquet garni, and serve.

Seasonings, Bouquets Garnis, Mirepoix and Clarified Butter

These are simple and lovely ways to gently heighten the flavors of soups, stews and other preparations.

The French introduced the bouquet garni, a small bundle of fresh aromatic herbs or vegetables tied together and tossed into the pot.

Then there are the sachets or herb pouches, which are made with dried herbs enclosed in little cheesecloth bags to keep them contained during cooking.

The usual method for making these clever flavoring devices is to enclose the fresh herbs or dry seasonings in a square of cheesecloth, draw the four corners together at the top and tie the cloth into a little pouch. Before serving, fish the pouch out with a slotted spoon or pull it out after tying a piece of string to connect the pouch and the pot handle. For smaller quantities, a tea ball comes in handy.

Always discard the seasonings before serving.

FRESH BOUQUET GARNI

1/2 bunch	fresh parsley, leaves and stems
3	whole bay leaves
1	medium-to-large sprig fresh thyme
1	celery stalk, including leaves, coarsely chopped

DRY BOUQUET GARNI

1	whole bay leaf
1 teaspoon	whole black peppercorns
1 teaspoon	dried thyme

SACHET D'EPICES NO. 1

3 or 4	fresh parsley stems with leaves, coarsely chopped
4	whole bay leaves
1/2 teaspoon each of:	dried basil
	dried oregano
	dried thyme

SACHET D'EPICES NO. 2

1/2 bunch	fresh parsley, leaves and stems, coarsely chopped
3	whole bay leaves
	medium-to-large sprig fresh thyme
1	celery rib, with leaves, coarsely chopped

WHITE MIREPOIX

1/2 cup	yellow onion, diced
1/2 cup	leeks, white parts only, washed well and coarsely chopped
1/2 cup	celery, diced
1/2 cup	parsnips, chopped
1	whole garlic head, cut in half horizontally
4	whole bay leaves

GREEN MIREPOIX

1/2 cup each of:	celery, coarsely chopped
	leeks, white and green parts, well washed and coarsely chopped
	green onion, coarsely chopped

Clarified Butter

Clarified or drawn butter is simply melted butter with the solids removed. Without these solids, clarified butter withstands high temperatures and maintains the delicate butter flavor. Clarified butter is also called butter oil.

DIRECTIONS

Over low heat, warm unsalted butter until it melts.

Remove from heat and let stand for a few minutes to allow the milk solids to settle to the bottom. Pour off the clarified butter oil into a container and discard the solids at the bottom. Keep cool.

OTHER SEASONINGS

CREOLE SEASONING

3 tablespoons	paprika
2 tablespoons each of:	onion powder
	garlic powder
	dried oregano
	dried basil
1 tablespoon each of:	dried thyme
	black peppercorns, freshly ground
	white peppercorns, freshly ground
	cayenne pepper
	kosher or sea salt, optional
dash each of:	chile powder
	cumin powder

SEAFOOD SEASONING

2 tablespoons each of:	granulated garlic
	granulated onion
	black peppercorns, freshly ground
1 teaspoon	dried oregano
1/2 teaspoon each of:	dried thyme
	white peppercorns, freshly ground
1/4 teaspoon each of:	dried basil
	cayenne pepper

POULTRY SEASONING

3 teaspoons	kosher or sea salt
1 teaspoon	paprika
1/2 teaspoon each of:	onion powder
	garlic powder
	black peppercorns, freshly ground
	white peppercorns, freshly ground
	cayenne pepper
	dried rosemary
	dried sage leaves
	dried oregano
	dried thyme

SEASONED SALT

3 tablespoons	kosher or sea salt
2 teaspoons	granulated sugar
1/4 teaspoon each of:	paprika
	onion powder
	garlic powder

INDEX

ACKNOWLEDGMENTS

New Orleans is a great food town, for both locals and visitors. For both, it's a love affair that never falters, and only becomes more passionate. This universal love of the city's restaurants is reflected in the appreciable increase in their number since Hurricane Katrina devastated New Orleans in 2005.

The New Orleans Classics series of cookbooks celebrates the contributions of dozens of chefs to the city's culinary reputation, as well as our appetite and gratitude for their efforts.

I'm especially grateful to Michael Lauve, a wonderful art director, and to Terry Callaway at Pelican Publishing Co., both of whom who made the production of the book a joy. My special thanks to Scott Campbell and Katie Szadziewicz of the Pelican team. Once again, Tom Groom gave us his all.

Gene Bourg, as editor, wrangled words and recipes in fairly good temper. Christopher Gromek worked as recipe tester, shopper and photo assistant—talents he has now fully developed. Elouisa Rivera backed him up, and chef Michael Shindle did his part. Chef Robert Barker weighed in on occasion with his valuable advice and expert cooking skills. Photographer Paul Rico continues to be my hero, and photographer David Spielman another talented source of advice. Patty Fox, my sister, cheerfully did her part.

As always, I own any omissions or errors. I'd enjoy receiving feedback about your results with the recipes. Please feel free to send any questions or comments to kit@kitwohl.com. In return, please don't send any chain e-mails, jokes or solicitations.

Friendship and support have been immeasurably valuable in this endeavor. Linda Ellerbee was there to prop me up when I was down, and provide the occasional reality check.

Finally, my gratitude goes to Billy, my love, to whom I say, "Your patience is stellar. And while your cooking is mostly limited to making soup and sandwiches and reheating take-out, your thoughtfulness is always appreciated."